The Official
F-19
Stealth
Fighter
Handbook

Richard G. Sheffield

COMPUTE! Books

Radnor, Pennsylvania

Acknowledgments

I owe all of the folks at MicroProse a great deal of thanks for producing such a fine product as *F-19 Stealth Fighter*. From Bill and Sid all the way down, you guys did a great job. In particular I'd like to thank Kathy Gilmore for constantly chasing down info and making sure I got to talk to the right people, Steve Meyer for telling me how they did it, and Chris Taormino for taking time out of his busy day to point out some of the finer details of the game to me.

Editor: Pam Williams

Printed in the United States of America

10 9 8 7 6 5 4 3 2

Sheffield, Richard G.
    The official F-19 Stealth Fighter computer game handbook / Richard G. Sheffield.
        p.   cm.
    Includes bibliographical references.
    ISBN 0-87455-217-6
    1. Computer war games. 2. Fighter plane combat. 3. Stealth aircraft. 4. Flight simulators. I. Title.
    U310.S465   1989
    358.4'148--dc20   89-42816
                                                                  CIP

COMPUTE! Books, Post Office Box 5406, Greensboro, North Carolina 27403, (919) 275-9809, is a Capital Cities/ABC, Inc. company and is not associated with any manufacturer of personal computers. *F-19 Stealth Fighter* is a trademark of MicroProse Software.

Contents

Foreword

Don't you just love flying? The way it makes you feel, the liberation of your feet from plain old, standard horizontal earth, the freedom to twist and turn and roll—all at hundreds of miles per hour? It's almost like being a kid at a playground again, spinning and zipping from here to there just for the sheer joy of motion.

I love flying so much that I went to the U.S. Air Force Academy to do it for a living. I graduated from the Academy in 1970 and have been lucky enough to get 3500 hours behind the stick in everything from trainers to A-37 jet fighters, and our company's own T-28 Trojan airplane, the lovely, charming, and talented Miss MicroProse. Flying has always been the most fun and exciting thing I ever wanted to do.

And am I ever excited about flying *F-19 Stealth Fighter!* Although we're always "pushing the envelope" of computer game technology, F-19 is the culmination of the great MicroProse tradition of authentic flight simulation. The tradition began in 1982 with *Hellcat Ace*, really took off with *F-15 Strike Eagle* in 1984, and blew people away in 1986 with *Gunship* and its solid-filled 3-D graphics. Now, I'm proud to say, "F-19 has the best 3-D graphics you've ever seen." They're the best in clarity, the best in detail, and the best in the sheer volume of neat things to see—cities, SAM sites, shipyards, ships, bridges, other planes, airbases—four whole worlds, each measuring 250 miles by 250 miles. That's a total of quarter-million square miles of real-world terrain.

My partner and computer game design genius Sid Meier is always mild-mannered and soft spoken, but during development even he occasionally revealed bubbles of enthusiasm for *F-19 Stealth Fighter*. The news of his breakthroughs spread quickly. From the early days of the project, everyone in the company, from the warehouse to the secretaries to the sales staff to the accounting department was buzzing with excitement. "Have you seen what they're doing? The graphics are unbelievable!"

But great graphics are only part of what makes *F-19 Stealth Fighter* such a magnificent game. After all, the terrain doesn't just sit there and look pretty. It's crawling with enemies and targets and hostile weapons carefully programmed to give you all the challenge you can handle. And as you choose higher and higher skill levels, the enemies get more experienced, better equipped and smarter—with artificial intelligence that will give your human intelligence a real run for its money.

Which brings up another big thrill for me in *F-19 Stealth Fighter*. Aside from the sheer fun of flying, I love to be in real situations where I have to make real decisions. I love games that require my intelligence, help me learn something about the real world, about my equipment, about the enemy's equipment, but mostly about myself. If you've played *F-19 Stealth Fighter*, you've probably learned a lot about yourself already. I'll bet your brain is running at Mach 5 when the bad guys start closing in!

F-19 has pulled in awards from all around the software industry. The one that makes me happiest, though, is the one from my peers. In May of 1989, *F-19 Stealth Fighter* won the Best Simulation Award from the Software Publishers Association. It means a lot when your friendly competitors say "Way to go, MicroProse!"

Another terrific honor is this book you're about to read. Rich Sheffield is one of the very finest and most knowledgeable journalists covering computer entertainment. The fact that he has developed the time and energy to write an entire book about F-19 Stealth Fighter is a tribute to the game's truly remarkable depth and sophistication—and fun! One of the nicest things he told me as he was researching the book is that "*F-19 Stealth Fighter* has the 'personality' the MicroProse games always seem to have."

That's a big compliment from a great writer who has written a terrific book about an outstanding game.

What more can I say? Only one thing: Good flying to you!

"Wild Bill" Stealey
President, MicroProse Software
Fighter Pilot

Introduction

Introduction

The MicroProse Story

Las Vegas, 1982. Another boring sales meeting would mark a drastic change in the lives of two very different men. Sid Meier and Bill Stealey were both working for the electronics giant, General Instruments Corporation. Stealey, the outgoing strategic planner, was directing the company's Business Development. Meier was an engineer and programmed minicomputers for the company's Business Systems division.

After a brief losing stint at the gaming tables one night, the two gravitated to the computer game arcade. The Atari 800 was a hot machine in the early 1980s, and both Stealey and Meier were avid computer gamers. As fate would have it, they found a stand-up Atari-based machine, Red Baron—an early, coin-operated flight simulator.

"Finally," thought Stealey, a former Air Force fighter pilot, "something in this town I can win at." But he was to be disappointed again. The confident fighter pilot challenged the quiet engineer to a couple of games. It didn't take the crafty Meier long to figure out the programming algorithms and top the fighter jock's scores. A frustrated Stealey, whose business cards still read "Fighter Pilot Supreme," complained the game was not realistic. Meier agreed and said he could do better than that in a week. Aware of a fighter pilot's love for fun and action, Stealey told Meier, "If you can, I bet I could sell this to every officers' club around the world."

Well, it took a little longer than a week (even this very first release was a little late due to Sid's insistence on perfection, a MicroProse tradition), but a couple of months later a smiling Meier walked into Stealey's office and handed him a disk. "Here it is; it's called *Hellcat Ace*," he said, and MicroProse was on its way.

The two men are totally opposite in personality, but they couldn't have made better business partners. To really understand how MicroProse has moved from the basement of Bill Stealey's house to a multimillion-dollar-a-year company, you

3

need to take a closer look at the two founders.

You never have to look around to know if Major "Wild Bill" Stealey is in the room with you. He always makes his presence known. Loud to the point of exuberance but not obnoxious, Stealey usually greets a newcomer with a big smile, a stiff handshake, and a challenge. Competition is a way of life for this young company president. Whether at trade shows or in the MicroProse offices in Hunt Valley, Maryland, Stealey seems always ready for quick session with their latest release. He's not only the president of MicroProse but the biggest fan of its games. Hours spent with a joystick in the evenings assure that he is always one of the best players of any game they release—and probably a few they don't. Stealey sets high goals for his products. If they don't live up, they don't go out.

He has always set high goals for himself, also, and seems to have a hard time understanding the word *no*. His military career is a good case in point. Early on he decided, like many young men, that being a fighter pilot looked like an exciting life. So he made up his mind he was going to be an Air Force fighter pilot and a general. But Stealey wore glasses, an instant disqualification for Air Force pilots. Most kids would have given up in the face of such a strict rule. I did. But he was more determined than most. While attending the Pennsylvania Military College, he kept after Air Force officials until he was given a rare waiver by the Air Force Academy. A minor slip-up in his final days dropped him to sixth in his class and out of the running for the fighter assignments. In consolation he took a post as a flight instructor, teaching young recruits to fly the T-37 jet fighter trainer.

Stealey had often bragged to his friends that he would make general by age 35. Several years in the service, however, showed him that if he was to make general, it would take a little longer, like 20 years or so. Impatient as always, his interests drifted to the business world, where he could run his own show a little sooner. An MBA from the Wharton School of Business soon followed, as did a job with one of the world's largest management consulting firms, McKinsey & Company.

While in business school, he finally reached his goal of being a fighter pilot. Many weekends were spent joyfully dropping bombs and firing missiles over the countryside of Pennsylvania and New Jersey with the Pennsylvania Air National Guard. During our first telephone conversation several years ago I mentioned that the Georgia Air National Guard unit near where I worked was transitioning from old F-4 Phantoms to sleek F-15 Eagles. Having piloted O-2 Skymasters and A-37 Dragonflies with the Air guard, he said that being able to fly an F-15 might be enough to tempt him to give up the president's chair for the ejection seat again. Spoken like a true fighter pilot.

While working at General Instrument directing company acquisitions, he met Sid Meier. Stealey had purchased an Atari 800 mainly to play *Star Raiders*, but he became more interested and joined Sid's newly formed users group. His association with Meier would eventually help him to achieve his second goal, that of becoming a general by age 35. Using the leadership skills pounded into him at the Air Force Academy and the business skills acquired at Wharton, he has developed MicroProse into a force any general would be proud to lead.

Sid Meier seems destined to work on computer games. Even as a child, his interest in science and history led him to dream up one game after another. His fascination with technology led to a Computer Science degree at the University of Michigan.

In 1980, Meier got into home computers when he purchased an Atari 800. He had taken an immediate interest in this computer because it had great graphics capabilities and supported a number of interesting games. Later that year he formed an Atari users group which eventually became known as SMUG, Sid Meier's Users Group. Later when Meier and Stealey were trying to decide on a name for their fledgling company, they almost chose Smuggers Software after Sid's group.

After his initial success with *Hellcat Ace*, Sid designed one game after another. With each release he honed his design skills and made the games more interesting and complex. During a time when everyone in the computer game industry was designing arcade style games, Meier continued to produce simulations with an emphasis on realism.

Sid's jet fighter game, *F-15 Strike Eagle*, was really the breakthrough release for MicroProse. It was an inspired design. Not only could the player fly a jet fighter, but now he could do battle against real countries. Flying missions against North Vietnam, Libya, and countries along the Persian Gulf kept players coming back again and again. This idea of using real geographic locations and enemies was to become a MicroProse trademark.

Sid's *Silent Service*, a World War II submarine simulation, was also a huge hit. In 1986 it was named the best simulation game in the U.S., England, West Germany, and France. In all, Sid's games have sold well in excess of two million copies world wide. When I asked Bill Stealey why he thought MicroProse had been so successful, he was quick to answer, "That's easy—Sid Meier."

The Making of *F-19 Stealth Fighter*

F-19 can trace its heritage back to a similar but different game MicroProse developed for the Commodore 64, *Project Stealth Fighter*. This game was popular on the Commodore, and the management at MicroProse had it scheduled for conversion to other machine formats. Previous conversions had led to minor improvements in the game play or graphics, but the games were basically identical across the various formats. But *F-19 Stealth Fighter* would be different.

About this time, it became obvious the game market was shifting in favor of the IBM compatible format and away from the Commodore 64/128, which had dominated the home market for years. This being the case, MicroProse was looking for a new hot game to really break into this format. So when Sid Meier (Senior VP and master game designer), Andy Hollis (3-D graphics ace), and Arnold Hendrick (game designer and documentation writer extraordinaire) came to Steve Meyer (VP of Product Development) and wanted to make some rather large improvements to *Stealth Fighter* for the IBM conversion, he was ready to listen. They wanted to improve the graphics, the game play—actually, just about everything.

But Steve Meyer also needed a new game and couldn't wait forever. He wanted to know if they could do it in a year.

Of course they said they could and immediately got to work.

It was a game designer's dream come true. They were given an already finished and popular game and given the chance to "do it over again," this time with more speed, power, and memory. It wasn't long before this previously minor conversion became a major development project. The team quickly grew as Jim Synoski, who helped design the C64 version, and David McKibbin were added. David's extensive IBM-compatible experience was a great help. He was able to write a number of graphics and operations "libraries" so the other programmers didn't have to know how all of the various IBM-compatible systems worked, they could just call the proper library file.

Other people were brought in, and the project grew and developed its own momentum. It was beginning to be obvious this game was something special. The 3-D databases for the "worlds" you fly in were redone and beefed up by Max Remington and Bruce Shelley, who managed to cram a lot of scenery into a small amount of memory. Murray Taylor added his expertise to the graphics as well. Ken Lagace came on board and did a superb job getting accurate and believable sounds out of a little speaker that was never intended for such things.

By this time, all of the top people at MicroProse from every department were working on this one project. Management was more than a little worried. But this was one of those situations where they just had to trust the team to do their best work and leave them alone. When there was something solid to work with, Al Roireau, Chris Taormino, and Russ Cooney started their Quality Assurance bug hunt, and Barabara Bents tried in vain to finalize the layout for the keyboard overlays.

The team had grown so large that Steve Meyer was forced to have regularly catered lunches so he could get the whole team together in one room to discuss progress and problems. The year they had to finish the project came and went, but they were allowed to continue work for several months before finally being forced to wrap the project up. So many things had been changed from the original C64 version that they decided to change the name and packaging to further distinguish it.

When *F-19 Stealth Fighter* hit the shelves in November of 1988, it was quickly apparent all of the hard work had been worthwhile. In its first 60 days on the market, *F-19* sold over 100,000 copies worldwide. Not only was it a hit, but it was well on its way to becoming one of MicroProse's biggest hits ever.

Rarely has a computer game attracted so much attention. Not only did it get rave reviews in the computer press, but it received wide coverage in publications such as *Time* magazine and *Popular Mechanics*. Even best-selling author Tom Clancy gave it a big thumbs up.

At the 1989 Software Publishers Association awards ceremony, *F-19* did what no other MicroProse hit had ever done: It won the Best Simulation of the Year award, an honor which many in the industry felt was too long in coming.

As if that wasn't enough, a modified version of *F-19* was the only computer game selected to be part of the exciting new exhibit at the National Air and Space Museum in Washington D.C. Entitled "Beyond the Limits: Flight Enters the Computer Age," this new exhibit will feature computers in aviation. The F-19 simulator is one of the highlights and offers visitors a true hands-on experience. Placed strategically next to the Space Shuttle Simulator, the F-19 exhibit will surely become one of the most popular attractions in America's most popular museum.

Chapter 1
Stealth Technology

1
Stealth Technology

An oddly shaped aircraft takes off from a lonely air strip in Turkey. Cruising low but not "in the weeds," the pilot guides his machine through the darkness towards the Soviet border. The mission profile is a familiar one, often conducted by the British and Americans. It's called "ringing the fire alarm." We want to know just how good the Soviet air defense system really is, so every now and then we "test" it. An aircraft is sent towards the border and all the sensitive intelligence gathering equipment we can muster is poised ready to scoop up data. All radar activity and communications in the area are carefully monitored. We want to know exactly when the aircraft is spotted, by which radar site, and which surface-to-air missile company is ordered to stand by.

It's a little game we play: How close can we get, how quick can they spot us. If we get a little closer than the last time, we win. If they spot us sooner and "sound the alarm," they win. But tonight, we're changing the rules. The pilot follows the normal flight plan, flying parallel to the border. He monitors the sensitive radar detection gear on board. Activity in the area is normal; he has not been spotted. In fact, his equipment shows his opponents aren't even close. Feeling comfortable, he starts phase two of the mission. A gentle turn to the north and he crosses into Soviet territory. Ever cautious and treading lightly, he doesn't want to awaken the sleeping bear; he just wants to nose around the cave a little bit.

He keeps a close eye on the SAM site just north of the small town of Brodilovo at the southwestern tip of Bulgaria. Radar emissions show an active SA-10 site in the area. He heads toward the site, watching for any change. The semi-active doppler radar scans the sky in a wide arc, looking but not seeing. The effective search range for this system is thought to be 320 km; the pilot smiles as he breaks 250 km. The smile disappears and he starts to sweat as he closes in on

11

120 km, well within the lethal range of the SA-10 Grumble missile. At 90 km the bear stirs. They still use the search radar, but the search arc has been narrowed to the pilot's little piece of sky. They know he's out there somewhere but can't get a good lock on. He checks his map; the Veleka river should be coming up soon. A quick check of the infrared imaging screen shows the dark black strip dead ahead. He lowers his altitude and turns to follow the river to the east. As he eases below 100 feet, the radar activity returns to normal—he simply disappeared. Even if they scramble a couple of MiGs to check it out, it's too late. Minutes later he passes over the Bulgarian shore and out over the Black Sea. Home free. We win this round without the opposition ever knowing they were playing the game.

There's good evidence to support that not only is a scenario like this possible, but that it has actually taken place, possibly many times. What makes this aircraft so different from the others which would be spotted well inside Turkey? It's stealth technology.

What Is Stealth Technology?

The use of the word *stealth* in the aerospace industry is a fairly recent occurrence. But it falls under a larger program that the military has been studying for a number of years—*Low Observability,* or *LO,* technology.

Most of the emphasis has been placed on the ability of stealth or LO aircraft to avoid radar detection, and rightly so, but to be truly stealthy, six areas must be taken into account.

- The *Infrared,* or heat, signature of the aircraft
- The *Acoustics,* or how much noise the aircraft makes
- *Visual appearance,* since the human eye is still a good detection device
- *Smoke emitted;* smoky engines point a large finger at the aircraft
- *Contrails,* or vapor trails left by the engines that must be reduced
- *Radar Cross Section,* or how well the aircraft can be seen on radar

Although all the others are important, dependence on high-tech radar for air defense makes the Radar Cross Section, or RCS, by far the most important area.

Radar Cross Section

Radar operates by sending out radar waves. When these waves strike an object, some of these waves are reflected back to the radar receiver and show up as a pip on the screen. The nature of these waves makes them operate in much the same way as bright sunlight on a highly polished surface such as an aircraft. No matter where you stand, there's some part of the aircraft that will reflect the sunlight directly at you. This is known as *glinting*. So when a normal aircraft is hit by radar waves, there is always some surface on the aircraft that will reflect these waves strongly back to the receiver.

Figure 1-1. Glinting and Facetting

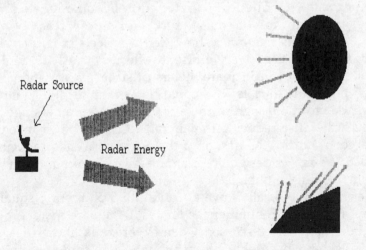

Radar Source

Radar Energy

Curved surfaces "glint" and reflect some of the radar energy back in all directions. Facetted surfaces reflect most of the radar energy in a single direction.

These surfaces may be broad, flat areas such as vertical stabilizers, which reflect most of the waves back in one direction. Or they may be curved surfaces such as wing edges or the aircraft body, which reflect the waves more or less equally in all directions, some of them glinting directly back to the receiver. These waves may also get stuck in cavities such as engine inlets. In this case, they'll resonate and send waves back in all directions.

In the early stages of radar development, researchers looked for a standard way to measure the ability of different objects to reflect radar waves. A standard call called the Radar Cross Section, or RCS, was developed.

The RCS for an object is calculated by first determining the amount of radar energy reflected by the object. Then calculations are made to determine the size of a reflective sphere that would reflect the same amount of radar energy. The area of a disk with the same diameter as the sphere is then the RCS for the object. The RCS is referred to in square meters.

It's important to note that the RCS for an object is not directly linked to its size but to how well it reflects radar waves. Broad, flat surfaces are very efficient reflectors. An F-15 Eagle fighter shows about 25 square meters of surface area when viewed broadside. But its RCS could be as high as 400 square meters, due to the design of the aircraft. Large numbers like this occur because reducing the aircraft RCS was never taken into account during the design of the airframe. When reducing the RCS is a major design criteria, amazing performance improvements can be obtained.

Jet fighters typically have a frontal RCS of about 6 square meters. Frontal RCS numbers as low as .01 square meters have been seriously discussed when experts talk about the stealth fighter. This would present roughly the same radar signature as a medium-size bird.

Reducing RCS

It might seem incredible to be able to reduce the radar signature of similar aircraft by so much. But once researchers discovered what made some aircraft reflect radar so well, they could set about reducing those items.

There are some treatments such as radar-absorbing paint and materials that can help to reduce RCS in normal aircraft, but the huge reductions in RCS are gained in changing the way we design airframes. Since the size and weight of the aircraft are not primary factors in RCS, the designer has some latitude in the way the aircraft is laid out. But some assumptions must be made up front. One assumption is that RCS from all angles cannot be reduced—there must be tradeoffs. If the main area of concern is the RCS when seen from the front and side, the RCS from top or bottom might not be so good. But that's a good assumption since few radars can look straight up or down. Another assumption: If this aircraft is going to depend on not being seen as a defense, it will not need to be as maneuverable as one that must hide in the terrain. This, too, gives the designer room to work.

With these items in mind, the designer can get to work. He must reduce broad, flat surfaces that would reflect back to the source. He must also eliminate as many right angles as possible. These usually occur where two items such as the wings and body meet. These right angles cause radar waves to be reflected from one surface to the other and then right back to the receiver, greatly increasing RCS. This is not to say that flat surfaces cannot be used, just that care must be taken to ensure that radar waves are not reflected back to their source.

The designer must also think ahead. If this is to be an attack aircraft, it must be able to carry weapons. If you hang a bunch of bombs and missiles under your carefully designed stealth aircraft, you're wasting time. The weapons will have as high an RCS as an entire airplane. So, the weapons must be carried internally until they're needed. This also goes for fuel. Since most fighters carry about 30 percent of their fuel in external tanks, these must be internalized as well.

Another method of reducing the RCS is the use of *RAM*, or *Radar Absorbing Materials*. These materials are composed of carbon and certain iron compounds, or salt-related polymers. These compounds have the ability to take the energy from a radar wave and convert it to heat. This heat is then easily dissipated by the aircraft. When these compounds are combined with nonreflective resin epoxies, they produce a material that's stronger than steel and 30-percent lighter than aluminum. This material can then be used as the skin of the aircraft or in the internal support structure.

Figure 1-2. Two Radar Absorbing Materials

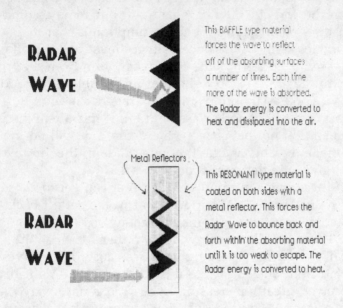

RADAR WAVE

This BAFFLE type material forces the wave to reflect off of the absorbing surfaces a number of times. Each time more of the wave is absorbed. The Radar energy is converted to heat and dissipated into the air.

Metal Reflectors

RADAR WAVE

This RESONANT type material is coated on both sides with a metal reflector. This forces the Radar Wave to bounce back and forth within the absorbing material until it is too weak to escape. The Radar energy is converted to heat.

All these items must be juggled to create an aircraft capable of avoiding radar detection, carrying enough weapons to be worth the trip, and possessing enough range to get somewhere useful. No easy task.

Stealth History

Since radar technology was developed during the Second World War, it should not be surprising to learn that the first attempts at stealth technology occurred during this period also. It might be surprising to learn, however, that it was the Germans, not the Allies, who worked on the project. The Germans were responding to the success the Allies were having with the early radar sets. Not only was their radar very effective at spotting incoming enemy bombers, but it was also very important in the battle for the Atlantic.

German U-Boat submarines were doing a very good job of disrupting the convoys carrying valuable supplies to England. The favorite tactic was to attack on the surface at night, often in large groups called *wolf-packs*. When radar appeared, this advantage was lost. In response, the Germans developed a radar absorbing paint. While this ferrite-based paint was much too heavy for aircraft, it could be used on submarines.

The United States' first stealth development was totally accidental and quickly forgotten. Shortly after the war, Northrop Aircraft developed an experimental bomber called the YB-49 Flying Wing. As the name implies, the aircraft had no body or tail; it was simply a large flying wing. The aircraft was assigned to perform a normal test flight over the Pacific. When the test was completed, they turned and headed for home, pointing the slim wing edge directly at the base radar station. The radar crew was shocked to see the aircraft suddenly appear almost overhead because they had seen no evidence of it on the radar screen. Interest in the project quickly faded after the bomber crashed in the Mojave Desert in 1948. The plane was very unstable in flight and this stability problem was listed as the cause of the crash. Ironically, the new top-secret B-2 Stealth Bomber bares a striking resemblance to this aircraft designed and built in the 1940s.

As radar equipment became more powerful and compact, the concept was all but forgotten. Emphasis was placed on developing faster aircraft, the theory being that the faster the aircraft was, the less time the radar operator would have to react to the threat. The problem with this line of thought was that as aircraft speeds increased, so did the size of the aircraft. The larger aircraft could be detected at greater distances, thus negating much of the speed advantage.

As bombers grew to the size of the B-52, it became apparent that something had to be done to reduce the effectiveness of enemy radar. Electronic jamming devices were developed to flood radar screens with returns, making it impossible to detect the source. The Quail pilotless decoy drone was also added to the B-52. This aircraft was designed to return a radar image as large as the B-52 bomber that carried it. This development is important in the history of stealth technology as it shows for the first time that the radar return of an aircraft does not depend on its size alone. The idea did not catch on right away, though, as the researchers concentrated on the development of more powerful jammers.

With the "cold war" and the Soviet Union well under way in the early 1950s, it became imperative that the U.S. should learn about military developments deep inside the country. Old bombers were converted to spy planes, but they soon proved to be very vulnerable to attack. In order to plug this intelligence gap, a new plane was designed. The idea was to create a plane that could cruise safely at very high altitudes, well out of the reach of any existing fighter. The design specification required that "consideration be given. . .to minimize the detectability by enemy radar."

The task of making this plane a reality fell upon the Advanced Development Projects team at Lockheed in California. This was a small team of highly qualified and highly motivated engineers and pilots. This highly secret facility became known as the "Skunk Works" and has been on the leading edge of stealth technology since the early 1950s.

The aircraft they developed became known as the U-2, and it was highly successful. The U-2 was the first aircraft to use radar-absorbing paint known as "Iron Ball." The aircraft was successful at penetrating Soviet airspace unobserved for a period, but it was known that eventually stronger radars and surface-to-air missiles would be developed. Of course, these systems were developed, leading to the shooting down of a U-2 and pilot Gary Powers.

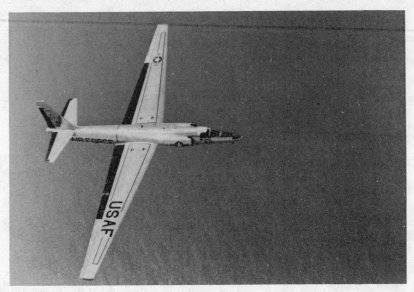

U-2 aircraft in flight over the Caribbean Sea.

Project Senior Crown

By this time, however, another aircraft was already being developed. It was to be capable of even higher altitudes and incredible speeds. Not only would it be able to fly higher than any enemy fighter, it would be able to outrun enemy surface-to-air missiles. It was soon realized an aircraft with these capabilities would have to be much larger than the U-2, which was basically a powered glider. This being the case, they would have to pay much more attention to reducing the RCS, or this larger target would be spotted as easily as the U-2. A low RCS was imperative; without it the extra performance would be meaningless. If the enemy could track the aircraft, they would simply cover all sensitive material in the area and the intelligence gathered would be of no use.

The design of the A-12 aircraft (later to be the SR-71) was based on low observability. Since no other aircraft had ever been developed with this in mind, it's not surprising the resulting aircraft looked unlike anything that had ever flown.

High-angle right-side view of a Strategic Air Command SR-71 aircraft, which can cruise at a speed in excess of 2,000 mph and an altitude above 80,000 feet.

The plane was long but slim. The engines were set into the wings, not under them, and the dual tail fins were slanted inward. All these items combined to form a very sleek aircraft with a trim profile.

There were other design items that weren't so easy to spot that also had a big impact on low observability. For the first time, radar absorbing materials other than paint were used. These materials covered the wing leading edges to reduce the glinting effect of curved surfaces. Flat areas such as control surfaces were also covered with the material to reduce reflections.

Despite all the high-tech advances made by project Senior Crown, political fallout from the Gary Powers incident was heavy. Before long, there were no more manned overflights of the Soviet Union. With the very mission it had been designed for now off limits, the ADP at Lockheed set about using the A-12 technology to design a pilotless vehicle. Project Senior Bowl produced the D-21 drone. It was designed to be dropped from another aircraft, probably an A-12 or B-52. It resembles one engine and the outer wing of the A-12. More extensive use of RAM and other stealth methods made this drone almost undetectable. The D-21 would be flown by radio into enemy territory to collect data. Once clear of the enemy border, it would drop the info by parachute. This chute would be snagged by another aircraft before it hit the ground. The drone would then self-destruct over the ocean, if possible. Little is known about the program except that few were used operationally and the aircraft was retired in 1972.

Stealth in Vietnam

The war in Vietnam posed a whole new set of problems to military planners. This was not a mechanized army we were up against but one that moved primarily at night, on foot and on bicycles—a very quiet army. Without the background noise of trucks and tanks, a recon plane overhead could easily be heard. Again Lockheed was contracted to produce an aircraft capable of performing reconnaissance undetected. At first, gliders were modified. Highly muffled engines and large, slow-turning props were added with great success.

This led to the development of the Q-Star and the YO-3. These aircraft were not very fast, had no armor, and were not very maneuverable. They were the first true stealth aircraft, as they relied totally on their ability to pass undetected behind enemy lines.

Many of these earlier developments would play an important role when it came time to develop the Stealth Fighter.

Chapter 2
The F-117A: The Real Stealth Fighter

2

The F-117A: The Real Stealth Fighter

In the late 1960s and early 1970s, it was becoming very clear to military planners that air defense systems all over the world were relying heavily on radar-based systems. The Linebacker I and II bombing raids into North Vietnam were dependent upon highly complex and expensive antiradar activities. On many missions, as many as one-third of all the aircraft involved were not carrying bombs for the target but were flying one of several missions to help foil enemy radar. First the Wild Weasels would go in to attack any operating radar sites. They would be followed by radar jamming aircraft, and then each bomber would drop huge amounts of chaff as it attacked the target. All this was an attempt to defeat radar.

Then, in October of 1973, war broke out again in the Middle East. In early air operations, the Israelis took a pounding from the SA-6 SAM missiles the Egyptians had acquired from the Soviets. Their jamming devices had been very successful against the older SA-2 and SA-3 systems but were not effective at all against the newer SA-6. Eventually, the U.S. provided effective jammers and the Israelis changed their tactics, but it was an unwelcome surprise.

It seemed clear jammers could be developed to counter almost any radar, but only after the new radar had been used successfully against you. Jammer development would likely lag behind radar development, always reacting and one step behind. This led researchers to seek out a completely new way of defeating radar that wouldn't be as susceptible to surprises.

Project Have Blue

Lockheed proposed the idea of developing a strike aircraft that would rely entirely on avoiding radar detection, as opposed to jamming the radar. The Stealth Fighter concept was born. The

Skunk Works received funding to produce a full-sized, proof-of-concept aircraft under Project Have Blue. Stealth being such a new concept, a small scale model would simply not do. To convince the skeptics, a full sized, operational aircraft was needed.

The team rapidly turned out the XST, Experimental Stealth Tactical prototype. The primary goal of the program was a very low radar cross section, particularly head-on. The XST was designed and built in Burbank, California, and transported deep inside the Nellis Air Force base in Nevada. The first XST flight took place at a portion of the Nellis facility know as Groom Lake in early 1977. The Nellis facility would be a very good location to test such an aircraft as it houses the Air Force's squadron of captured Soviet aircraft. These include MiG-23s, SU-20s, and probably a few newer MiGs they haven't publicly admitted to having. Also at Nellis are quite a few real and simulated Soviet-built SAM radar systems. With this type of equipment available, they could test their stealth theories against the real thing. The project must have been a success, as they quickly received funding to develop an operational Stealth Fighter.

This success gives the U.S. a very real advantage over the Soviets. It forces them to spend a great deal of money to develop new radar systems for air defense, with no guarantee that even the new systems will be effective as radar-avoiding technology continues to develop.

THE F-19?

Under a Special Access, or "Black," program named *Senior Trend*, 67 aircraft were built and delivered to Nellis where a new Air Force unit, the 4450th TG, was based.

Many in the press and industry assumed the Stealth Fighter had been designated the F-19 since the Air Force had not announced an aircraft between the F-18 Hornet and the F-20 Tigershark. Officials denied this, saying the F-19 designation had not been used to avoid confusion with the MiG-19. But when a later aircraft was designated the F-21 despite the large number of MiG-21s around, this argument was discarded. For some unknown reason, Lockheed and the Air Force reverted back to the old 100 series of fighter numbers. The actual designation turned out to be the F-117A. As of this writing it hasn't been given an official nickname such as the F-15 Eagle or F-14 Tomcat, but the name Nighthawk is being used by some industry writers.

Figure 2-1. F-117A Stealth Fighter

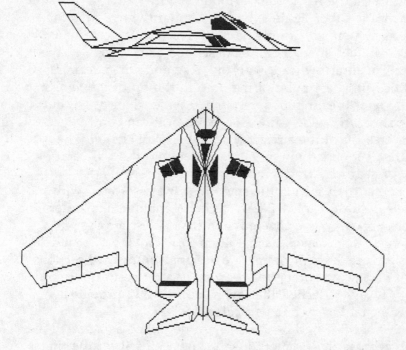

The first F-117A flew at Groom Lake in June of 1981. After trials and testing it became an operational aircraft in the Air Force inventory in October 1983.

The 4450th TG gathered many of the best pilots from units all over the world. Mostly they sought pilots with Wild Weasel or F-111 Strike experience. This gives us a not-so-subtle hint as to the expected mission of the F-117A. No volunteers were requested; rather, the Air Force chose to "invite" certain handpicked candidates. They were told little about the project other than they were being offered an opportunity to participate in one of our nation's most important defense programs. Those who accepted became part of the 4450th and were tasked with learning how to fly a most unusual aircraft.

Basic Design

Most fighter aircraft are very good radar reflectors; since the F-117A was designed to avoid radar detection, it follows that it would bear little resemblance to other fighter aircraft. It's similar in size to other fighters, but the similarity ends there. It's short as fighters go, at only 35 to 40 feet with a wide wingspan of 45 feet or so. It can be described as boxy and shaped rather like an arrowhead, with the nose and wings forming a solid line from the point of the nose to the tip of the wings. The body of the aircraft is very much wider than usual, but being short and wide with a flat bottom, it can contribute to the overall lift of the aircraft. The single pilot sits under a canopy that is blended in a pyramid shape into the nose and body of the aircraft.

Rather than having the smooth shape associated with the models of the F-19, the F-117A is quite angular. The outer surface appears to be covered with RAM tiles in a system known as *cut-diamond*. Each section forms a "facet" that's designed to break up incoming radar signals into small sections and reflect what cannot be absorbed in a different direction. This way any reflection that might occur won't provide a strong signal to any one particular receiver.

The old Boeing XB-47 was often described as a sacred airplane because the reaction of someone seeing it for the first time was "Holy Smoke!" Similar reactions must frequently occur with the F-117A.

Range

Specific information about the operational range of the F-117A is quite classified. The wide body houses two modified General Electric F404 engines, without reheat or afterburners. This and its size suggest a gross weight of about 45,000 pounds, with a payload capability of 4000 to 5000 pounds. The wide body should have a good deal of room for fuel cells, and fuel consumption rates should be low since the aircraft doesn't have to hug the ground and constantly maneuver. Add to this that it has been reported Oliver North developed a plan to use the F-117A in the retaliatory raid on Libya in 1986, and you can guesstimate a range of about 800 nautical miles.

In the North scenario, the F-117A would have been carried in a C-5 transport plane to a base in either Spain or Sicily. It would then fly the round trip to Tripoli over water. The plan was shot down by the joint chiefs of staff as being too risky. But the fact that the Air Force would be the only participant in the raid probably had something to do with the decision. As it turned out, the Air Force and Navy "shared" the strike. Actual military action is called for very rarely, so when it does come, everyone wants in on the act.

There's a debate over the aircraft's ability to be refueled in the air. Some say this is so important as to be a main design specification. Others contend the F-117A will rely on its remarkable combat range to perform almost any mission without needing to refuel. Since large circling tankers are easily spotted on radar, they might point to the possible intended path of the Stealth Fighter, making interception easier. Most tankers would be tied up with fighter and bomber missions in wartime, so the F-117A would likely need to rely on internal fuel for most missions.

Wobbly Goblin

With such an unconventional shape, the F-117A almost certainly use a fly-by-wire system. Such a system would let an onboard computer make hundreds of minute flight corrections a second to keep the aircraft stable. Even so, some report it's not an easy plane to pilot. *Time* magazine reported the pilots had nicknamed the plane the Wobbly Goblin due to its somewhat frightening handling characteristics. Others say that, while this may have been true at one time, the plane flies better than it looks and probably better than you might think.

Even so, the weight of the vehicle compared to the amount of lift produced doesn't reveal a very maneuverable aircraft. It should be just fine for strike and reconnaissance missions, but it wouldn't do well in a high-energy dogfight with a conventional fighter. True to its name, this Goblin would likely enter enemy territory unseen, attack, and leave the same way. Enemy aircraft encountered along the way would be avoided if possible.

Weapons

Since most weapons and their racks are excellent radar reflectors, all weapons will be carried internally in two weapons bays. A wide variety of weapons could be fitted into the retractable weapons platforms, but the most popular will probably be the AGM-65 Maverick missile.

Antiradar missions would call for the use of either the Shrike or HARM antiradiation missiles. A third possibility would be to carry the recently disclosed AGM-135A Tacit Rainbow antiradiation drone. This weapon is similar to the HARM, but it also has an internal engine. It would home in on radar signals and destroy the source or loiter over a given area waiting for the radars to be turned on.

Another option is the newly designed BLU-109 Paveway III Laser Guided Penetration Bomb. This 2000-pound bomb is designed to penetrate and destroy six feet of reinforced concrete. As noted aviation author Bill Sweetman recently told *Popular Mechanics* magazine, "By using unclassified DOD literature, one can trace exactly what type and how many of a given weapon system are being supplied to a known Air Force unit. Strangely, there are no records available on the distribution of the BLU-109/B. You figure it out."

Very little is known about the weapons targeting system. The only released photo shows a circular opening just below the base of the cockpit on the nose of the aircraft. It's believed this is the sensor module for weapons targeting. These systems would likely include forward-looking laser radar, forward-looking infrared, and a special low-light television system. Since this opening would have a similar field of view as the pilot, there may be a helmet-linked aiming system similar to the one used in the AH-64 Apache helicopter. With this system, all the pilot has to do to aim a weapon is look at the target.

Infrared and Visual Detection Avoidance

The infrared, or heat, signature of the aircraft has been reduced in several ways. First, several bypass systems are used to mix exhaust gases with cool air so these gases are cooler when they leave the aircraft. They're also vented above the wings to reduce the signature from the ground. Most IR-seeking missiles seek the hot exhaust nozzles, not the hot gases themselves, so special materials were used to keep these nozzles from heating up. Even so, there are new generation IR-seeking missiles that can detect even the hot leading wing edges from head-on. To counter this, reinforced carbon fibers that resist heating are used on most leading edges.

Visual avoidance is the subject of much speculation. There has been talk of "active background masking" techniques where the aircraft would have the ability to change colors to effectively blend in with its background, much like the alien in the movie "Predator." While such a system would be very valuable, it's also highly unlikely. More likely is the standard flat black for nighttime and dull gray for daytime flights.

F-117A vs. F-19

The F-19 Stealth Fighter envisioned by MicroProse and many others was a much larger, harder-hitting aircraft. But due to its size, the F-117A is probably more maneuverable. It's probably faster also, since both designs are said to use GE F404 engines, although it's hard to see how they could be crammed into the small airframe of the F-117A.

This small airframe would be a definite plus for stealth design. Since it would be much lighter, more nonreflective composite materials could be used. The F-117A would be much harder to spot either with radar or the human eye than the larger F-19.

Avionics are probably similar. At $60 million or so each, the F-117A should have the very latest in avionic and targeting equipment. This would include items seen on the F-19 such as targeting cameras, Forward-Looking Infrared sensors for night activity, laser target designators, and situation awareness maps and displays.

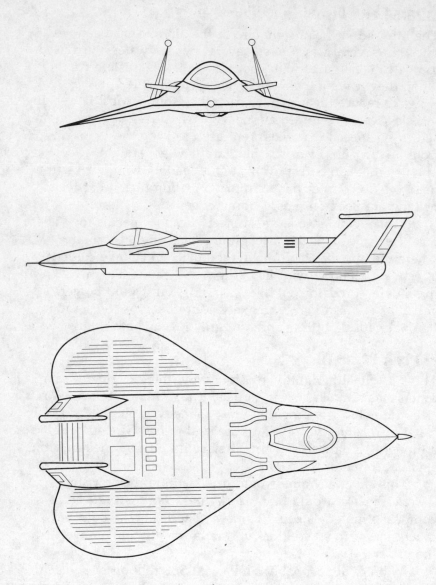

The F-19 Stealth Fighter, as pictured here, was envisioned to be bell-shaped, with a few sharp angles, and having inward canted stablizers.

The F-19 has four internal weapons bays, the F-117A only two. Consequently, the F-19 would be able to take out a large number of targets on a single mission. The F-117A would be limited to one or two sites.

Other New Stealth Aircraft

Besides the highly publicized B-2 Stealth Bomber, there are currently several other ongoing stealth-related projects. There's one school of thought that insists the RF-19 still exists as something very different from the F-117A. It would closely resemble the F-19 design seen in this game and elsewhere.

Lockheed is also said to be working on another stealth aircraft, the Aurora, a hypersonic reconnaissance plane designed to replace the aging fleet of SR-71s. This aircraft, also built at the Lockheed Skunk Works facility in Burbank, would be capable of almost Mach 6, operate on liquid methane, and have an effective range of almost 6,000 miles. There are reports of sighting this aircraft at the Nellis-Groom Lake facility also. Reports of this aircraft's existence are aided by the fact that the Air Force has been reducing the number of SR-71s over the past several years. Surely they're being replaced with something. Chance are, it's already operational. With the old SR-71, the Soviets knew we were there; they just couldn't do much about it. With the new Aurora operating stealthily at 150,000 feet and Mach 6, they might never know we're there at all.

Other stealth programs about which little is known are the Northrop Tactical Stealth Aircraft project, and the General Dynamics Model 100.

3
Flying the F-19

It's fairly obvious from just looking at it that the F-19 is no ordinary fighter plane. Though it's not that difficult to fly, you certainly have to fly in a much different manner than you would in a conventional fighter. Flying a stealth-type mission is very unforgiving, so it's imperative to think through your actions and to have a plan. Knowing what you want to do well ahead of time will allow you to accomplish your task in a smooth manner. A light hand on the controls and smooth flying is the key to success with *F-19*.

F-19 Flight Characteristics

First off, the F-19 was not built to outfly, or for that matter to outrun, anyone. Keep this in mind when planning your missions. The aircraft has two large engines, but without reheat (afterburners) it cannot power its way out of trouble. You must keep an eye on your airspeed.

Since the aircraft is basically underpowered, you need to be very careful when performing maneuvers. Steep climbs bleed off airspeed in a hurry and also present a large radar target. If you must climb, do it gradually. This way you can preserve your airspeed, keep engine output low, and keep your radar profile low.

Hard turning presents a similar set of problems. Banking angles of more than 45 degrees causes the stall speed to increase dramatically. In normal flight, your stall speed is about 100 knots or so; in a very steep turn it may go over 250 knots. So you could be cruising nicely at 190 knots with no problems, but if you turn quickly to avoid a missile you could stall, even without losing any airspeed.

Figure 3-1. Turning Increases Stall Speed

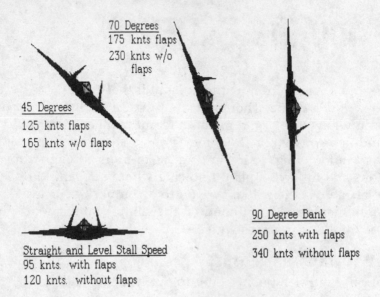

70 Degrees
175 knts flaps
230 knts w/o
flaps

45 Degrees
125 knts flaps
165 knts w/o flaps

90 Degree Bank
250 knts with flaps
340 knts without flaps

Straight and Level Stall Speed
95 knts. with flaps
120 knts. without flaps

Any time it looks like you may get into a scrap, it's a good idea to take a quick look at your airspeed. If it's below 200 knots, you might want to add a little throttle. If you're about to get into a tough dogfight, it's probably a good idea to give it full power. If the enemy isn't already tracking you, it will be shortly after a hard turn or two gives them a large radar profile. Given this, you might as well use all the power available.

This isn't to say the F-19 can't turn well—it can. It has a very good initial turn rate, but it cannot sustain that rate for very long without a stall. Keeping the nose up during a turn might keep you from stalling, but it also causes you to gain altitude. The higher you get, the better you can be seen, but sometimes there's no alternative.

Maintaining a Good "Stealth" Profile

Low and slow, smooth and smart. Keep that phrase in mind as you fly. The lower the better; 100 to 150 feet is good. It gets a little rough down there, but extending the flaps will smooth things out somewhat. Use of the flaps may increase your RCS slightly, but when you're down this low it really shouldn't matter.

Your ideal speed will depend upon your situation. When you're not near the enemy, you might want to cruise at high speed to get to the target area faster. But once you begin to close on enemy radar sites or aircraft patrols, slow down. Again, the slower the better. You can cut the throttle to 30 or 40 percent and still stay airborne by extending the flaps and pulling the nose up. Flying this slowly will get you nowhere in a big hurry, but you'll be very hard to spot. By flying low and slow, you'll be able to fly right under many enemy air patrols. But if you're spotted, remember to keep an eye on your airspeed as you respond. Avoid the urge to turn hard and engage the fighters until you add throttle and increase your speed. Turning hard at such a low airspeed without adding power will quickly result in a stall and, if you're at low altitude, this stall will quickly result in a very stealthy smoking hole in the ground.

Figure 3-2. Fly Low and Slow

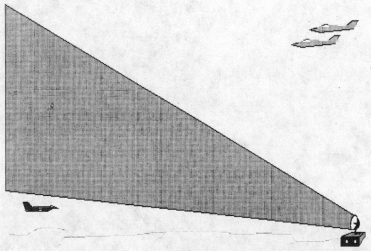

Staying below 200 feet and under 200 knots will let you pass safely under many enemy air patrols and a lot of radar coverage.

Fly smoothly, and try to avoid steep turns or climbs. Turning hard will greatly increase your radar profile, so take it easy and think ahead. Start your turns early so you don't need a steep angle. This is especially true for flying at a low airspeed.

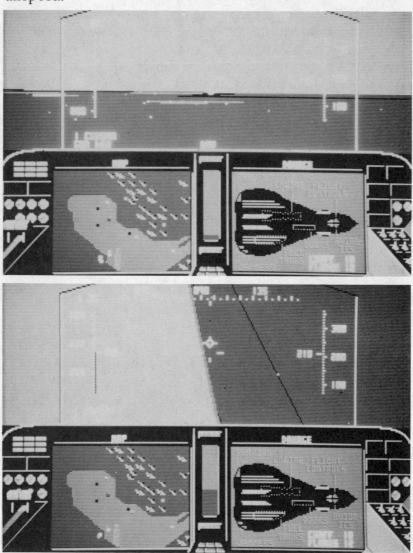

While flying straight and level, your EMV hugs the bottom of the scale (the bar indicator in the middle of the instrument panel). But a hard turn at the same speed sends your EMV almost halfway up the gauge.

Fly smart. You're given a great deal of information in the cockpit, so learn to use it. You know that turning will increase your profile, so if you're close to being spotted, time your turn between radar pulses. The situation map and the EMV scale will show each time a radar site pulses toward you. Watch them for a minute to get the period between pulses. This can be very effective when flying near Pulse-type radar sites. These sites can be fooled by flying straight toward or straight away from them. By timing your turn, you can fly deep into the radar coverage area then turn hard between pulses to head away in another direction. Keep an eye on other radars in the area. Don't be so concerned with avoiding one that another sees you in the process. Flying smart means using the terrain as cover when it's available. It may take you out of your way somewhat, causing you to use more fuel, but if you can make the transit safely by flying in a canyon or behind a mountain, you'll likely save fuel: Twisting and turning to avoid SAMs and enemy fighters will burn up a lot more fuel than flying a little farther nice and smoothly behind a mountain.

Takeoffs and Landings

Most players don't seem to have much of a problem with takeoffs, so I won't spend much time on them here. But there's one thing you might want to remember: The F-19 has a center of gravity that's well to the rear of the aircraft. Because of this, on takeoff the nose will come up well before the aircraft has enough speed to lift the rest of the plane. So don't assume that just because the nose will lift you're ready to rotate and fly. Keep an eye on the stall indicator bar on the left side of the HUD; don't try and lift off until the bar is below the middle indicator.

Quite a few people I talk to, both online and in person, seem to have trouble landing. In order to get those really high scores, you're going to have to learn to operate in the Realistic Landing mode. I'll try and cover landing procedures in some depth.

Getting Lined Up

The most important, and difficult, part of learning to land is

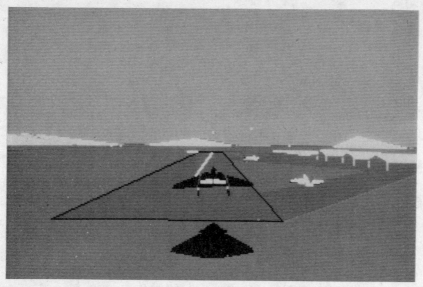

Once you learn the process, safe landings are no longer a problem.

learning how to get properly lined up with the runway. Imagine that the runway isn't a short concrete strip but a straight highway that extends for miles to the north and south. (Remember all runways and carriers in *F-19* are lined up pointing north-south.) This is a long and wide highway, but you can only land on the portion near the base. If this were the case, getting lined up would be easy—you could just fly over to this highway, turn, and follow it all the way back to the base. You'd be perfectly lined up. Learning how to use a couple of the instruments you have on board will allow you to do this.

When you first learn to land, the Instrument Landing System (ILS) may be more confusing than helpful, so I'll cover it later. For now we won't use it.

You need to start thinking about getting lined up early; 50 km isn't too soon.

Landing Procedure

An example is the best way to explain the landing procedure.

Here's the setup. You can recreate this setup and follow the procedure with the game. I'm flying the Strike Training

Mission against Libya off the USS *America.* I've completed my mission against Tripoli, and its time to head home.

• I'm heading due north, 000 degrees, north of Tripoli over the Mediterranean Sea. My INS cursor at the top of the HUD is pointing to the last waypoint. My assigned landing location, Sigonella Airbase in Sicily.

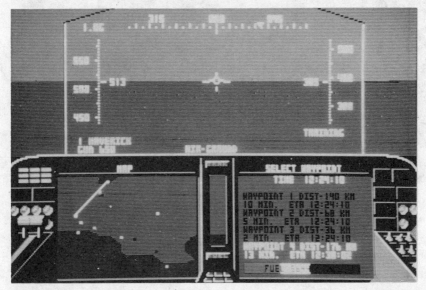

Mission over and headed for home.

• Once I'm clear of the enemy, I want to get set up to make an approach into Sigonella on a heading of 000 degrees. The HUD cursor shows the base to be slightly to my right. A heading of 20 degrees would take me straight to it, but I would come in crooked to the runway. I want to come in on a heading of 000. So, to correct this, I start my setup by turning to my right and taking a straight and level course of 90 degrees.
• I maintain this heading until the cursor moves all the way to the left of the scale. Now I should be approximately due south of the base. You can verify this on the Situation Display. You may still be too far away to pick up the base on the Trackcam.

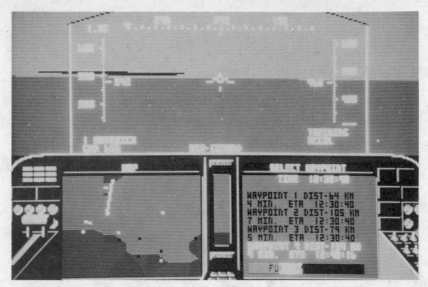

To start the lineup process, I fly at a 90-degree heading until the HUD NAV cursor hits the edge of the scale.

- Now I turn to the left and make my heading 45 degrees. You should be able to see the 000 heading indicator now. If not, maintain this heading until you can.
- I maintain a heading of 45 degrees until the cursor is just one major division to the right of the 000 heading indicator. I start a shallow turn to the right. Note that both the cursor and the 000 heading indicator start to move toward the center of the scale. The 000 indicator should move faster. My goal is to time my turn and my pull out so the cursor and the 000 indicator both arrive at the middle of the scale at the same time.

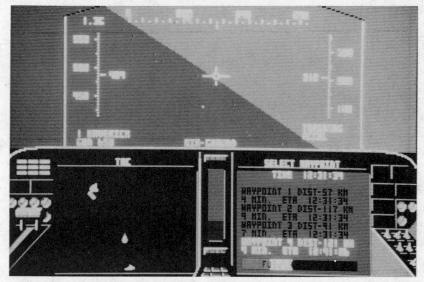

I turn towards the base and try to time my turn so the NAV cursor and the 000 heading indicator both arrive at the center of the HUD at the same time.

• It appears the cursor will get to the center first, so I level out for a minute and the cursor will start to move slowly away from the center, letting the 000 indicator catch up. Turning back to the left for a minute or two will speed up the process.

• So now I'm on a heading of 000 and the cursor is in the middle of the scale. I know I'm heading directly toward the base (because the cursor is in the middle), and I know the runway is lined up on a 000 heading—my heading is 000, so I must be correctly lined up!

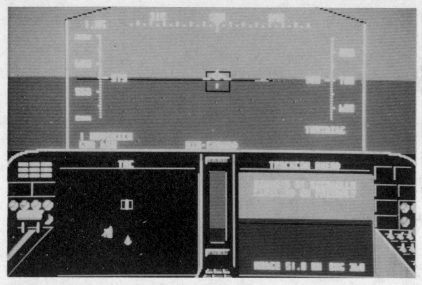

I level the wings on a heading of 000 and with the NAV cursor in the center of the scale. Perfectly lined up!

- By starting early and making small adjustments, you should be able to get lined up even before you pick up the base on the Trackcam at 50 km. **Note:** Don't be fooled by the airstrip at Halfar. It will show up first on both the Trackcam and the Situation Display. The base you want is Sigonella, which is to the northeast of Halfar.
- OK, I'm all lined up and I've got Sigonella on the Trackcam 45 km away. I level out at 500 feet.
- At 20 km, I cut back on power to bring my airspeed down below 250 knots. I also extend the flaps.
- At 15 km, I can get a good look at the runway on the Trackcam. I'm a little off, but not enough to worry about. The runway is very wide. I'll have plenty of room to land a little crooked.

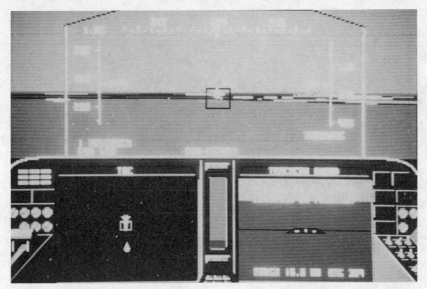

Fifteen kilometers out, my speed is coming down. I extend my flaps and check my lineup.

- At 10 km, I cut my power a little more to bring it down to less than 200 knots and lower the landing gear.
- Lowering the gear causes me to start to descend slightly; I keep my nose up slightly and let her lose altitude.
- At 2 km out I get to 100 feet. This puts me short of the runway, so I pull back on the stick a little to hold my altitude at 80 feet.
- At 1 km, I ease forward on the stick and start to descend again. Note that my nose is still pointing slightly upward; I'm not diving for the runway.
- As I cross the end of the runway, I'm down to ten feet and I cut power. The wheels touch the ground and I tap the brake key once (do not hold it down). I'm a little crooked, so I steer to the left as the plane rolls to a stop. Another successful mission!

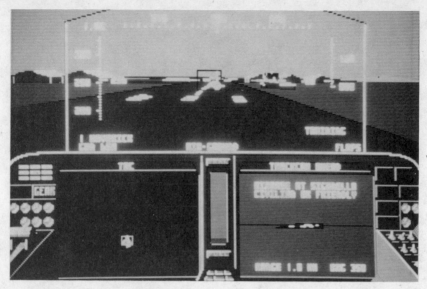

I cross the end of the runway at ten feet and cut power, keeping the nose up.

Coming in on such a shallow glide path isn't the way they teach it in flight school, but it's a good way to begin to learn about landing with this game. As you become more proficient, you'll want to land at a higher speed and use the steeper glide slope indicated by the ILS. "Tail dragging" landings as described above aren't good form, but if you're having trouble getting your bird safely on the ground, it's a good place to start.

A nice, smooth, touchdown!

The ILS

The Instrument Landing System (ILS) comes in very handy when trying to learn the proper glide slope for a good military landing. I prefer to use the above method for getting lined up and then level out at 500 feet. With the ILS on, I wait for the glideslope bar (the horizontal part of the T) to start to descend. As it crosses the center of the scale, I nose down a little to try and keep in the middle. The ILS will shut off as you get close to the runway. From that point you're on your own, so be ready.

The ILS is most useful when making a carrier landing. Here the glide slope is very important. If you come in too shallow, it's hard to see the deck and judge where to touch down. Of course, if you come in too steep you'll make a real mess on the deck. The same will happen if you try and land from the wrong direction. Remember, when you're coming in from the right direction, the carrier "island" will be on the right-hand side of the deck.

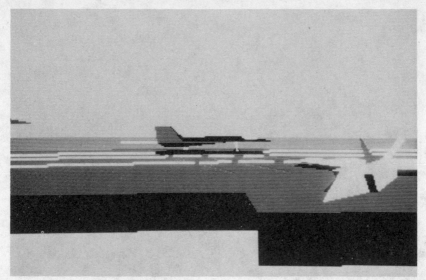

Remember to add full power just as you touch down on the carrier deck, just in case you miss the cables.

Following the indicated glidepath for a carrier landing is a little frightening at first. It looks like you're coming in awfully steep, but it works well once you get used to it. Since a carrier landing is really a controlled crash, you're allowed to hit the deck much harder than if you were landing on a runway. Just remember to pull the nose up as you land and to add full power in case you miss the cable and have to go around. Doing touch and go landings on a carrier deck can be quite a thrill!

Punching Out

Sometimes you have no other choice but to "hit the silk" and bail out. During that first instant when you realize you no longer have control of the aircraft is when you must fight the panic and evaluate the situation. Of course, there are situations that require no evaluation. If you loose control at low altitude and low speed, you had better get out in a hurry! But if you have some time, you may improve your odds by thinking for a second. If you're above 14,000 feet (not a good idea to

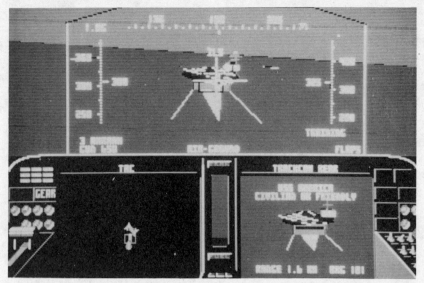

Following the glidepath indicated by the ILS may seem a little steep, but you are allowed to hit a carrier deck much harder that you could hit a runway.

begin with), ride the aircraft down for a while until you're at a lower altitude.

What happens to your plane after you leave it is also important. Letting this top secret weapons system fall into enemy hands will be bad news even if you're rescued or eventually released. So your best bet is to get your crippled bird as far out to sea as possible—well over deep water. If you ditch here, you have a great chance of being picked up by friendly forces, and the debris of your plane will be gone forever.

Bailing out over friendly territory is the next best thing, though some of the aircraft debris could still fall into the wrong hands.

Bailing out over enemy territory or close to an enemy shore should be avoided if at all possible. Not only will you be captured and put through a humiliating trial, but the enemy will be able to learn a lot from the crash site. Even if you're eventually released, such an incident will definitely throw a wet rag on your career as a military pilot.

Chapter 4
Air-to-Ground Tactics

4
Air-to-Ground Tactics

Missions involving air-to-ground action, whether it's bombing or photographing, are the reason the Stealth Fighter was developed. Sure, there are times when air-to-air missions might be called for and it certainly must be able defend itself, but there are many other aircraft much better suited to the air-to-air role.

Accurately delivering air-to-ground weapons requires skill, practice, and knowledge. The symbology used on the Heads-Up Display (HUD) will change with various types of weapons, so you should practice in training mode with all of the various weapons. By doing this, you'll know what to expect when you start your approach to the target. Few things can ruin a bombing run quicker than the appearance of a bunch of unfamiliar symbols on your HUD.

HUD Symbology

There are three basic HUD setups for air-to-ground targets, which correspond to the four different types of air-to-ground ordnance carried by the F-19.

Guided Missiles. Since guided missiles use their own internal systems to lock onto and steer towards the target, they're the easiest to use. The symbols on the HUD are also simple. When the target is acquired, the normal target indicator box will appear. Once the target is within the maximum range of the weapon, this box changes into an oval. If you have to, you can fire the missile at this point. But the weapon will have a much better chance of hitting the target if you wait until the oval changes color. Once this occurs, your chances of scoring a hit are better than 90 percent.

Laser Guided Bombs. These weapons are very easy to use since they're also self-guided, homing in on the refraction of a laser, which is pointed at the target from your fighter. This type of ordnance is dropped in a similar manner as guided missiles. The target indicator box will come up as before. Once in range, the box will change to an oval. This may change colors as before (if it does, it will happen very quickly) or it may come up already indicating that it's at the maximum accuracy level, depending upon your setup. Once this occurs, open the bay doors and drop the bomb.

Since the weapon is guided by a laser carried in the belly of your aircraft, you must remember to keep the belly of the plane pointing towards the target until the bomb impacts. This doesn't mean you can't turn away after you drop; in fact, if you're below 3000 feet, you had better turn away or you'll be caught in the bomb blast. But don't turn too hard.

Retarded Fall Bombs. Here's where things start to get a little tricky. Since these bombs are unguided, you must drop them at precisely the right moment if you're to hit the target. Your onboard computer takes care of the calculations and gives you all the information you need up on the HUD.

The first indicator you need to be aware of is the *Ranging Bar*. This bar extends across the top of the HUD display as soon as you arm the weapon. Once a target is locked, the ends start to move toward the center of the screen. You want to be ready to drop the weapon when the two ends meet.

While you watch the Ranging Bar, you should adjust your flightpath using the *Bombsight Flightpath Guide*. This small diamond-shaped symbol indicates the proper flightpath for you to take to overfly the target. The small circle in the center of the HUD shows your current flightpath. You should align the circle with the diamond to take the correct course.

Note: The diamond can be above or below the circle and not affect your accuracy, but being to the left or right will most likely cause a miss.

Since timing is so important when using this type of ordnance, approaching the target at low speed will make it easier to release the bomb at just the right moment.

Free-Fall Bombs. The HUD setup for free-fall bombs is basically the same as for retarded fall bombs with the addition of the *Bombsight Fall Line* and the *Bombsight Bullseye*. These items show where the bombs will land but really aren't important in the aiming and dropping process.

Dropping free-fall bombs can be dangerous for two reasons. First, they must be dropped from high altitude, which will expose you to radar detection and all the bad things that follow. Secondly, they travel at about the same speed as your aircraft. So if you continue to fly over the target after release and you're too low, you'll be right above the target when the bomb hits and you'll get caught in the blast. For these two reasons, and since they're hard to use anyway, I recommend you avoid carrying them if at all possible.

Strafing Ground Targets

One weapon you always carry is often overlooked in the ground attack mission: the 20mm cannon. Learning how to successfully strafe a target is very important if you want to increase your scores in Conventional War. Strafing requires practice, but once mastered it can be an invaluable skill. Never again will you be forced to pass by good targets because you're out of bombs and missiles. The real key is to establish a set procedure and follow it every time until it becomes second nature. The following sequences works well for a number of players.

- Line the target up early. Once you start to dive on the target, it's too late to make major course changes. So take the time to make sure you're perfectly lined up as you approach the target.
- Approach the target at low altitude until the range to the target is 6 km. This way you can avoid detection until the last possible moment.
- At 6 km, pull up hard, being careful to maintain a straight course. Level out at 1000 feet or so; the exact altitude isn't important. You just want to make sure you have enough room to dive on the target. As your skill improves, you'll find you require less altitude and can start your attack from 500–800 feet.
- Your gun is most effective when the range is less than 3 km. So at 3 km, extend your speed brake and start to dive on the target. Put the aiming circle either directly on the target or just a little in front of it. Fire a short burst and watch where

the shells land. Make minor adjustments and continue to fire short bursts.

- Pull up as soon as you hit the target or if you get below 150 feet. As you gain experience, you'll be able to judge when to pull up by the size of the target, which will get larger as you approach the ground. DON'T WAIT TOO LONG before you pull up. Most targets you would strafe are only going to give you a few points. Don't get so involved that you fly into the ground while trying to destroy a 30-point target.

Figure 4-1. Strafing

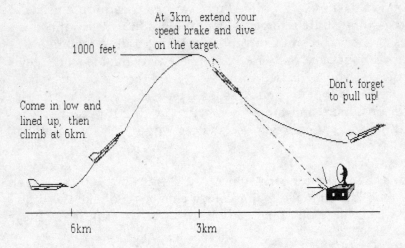

At 3km, extend your speed brake and dive on the target.

1000 feet

Don't forget to pull up!

Come in low and lined up, then climb at 6km.

6km   3km

Gun Accuracy

The accuracy required to destroy a target increases as you move up in difficulty levels. In other words, it's much easier to successfully strafe a target when playing against Green troops than it is playing against Veteran or Elite level troops.

At the Green troops level, all you have to do is get close to the target and it will be destroyed. At Elite level, you really have to hit the bullseye.

Figure 4-2. Gun Accuracy

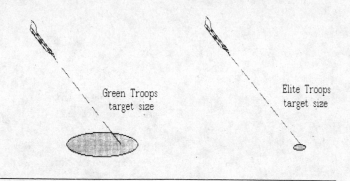

As you increase the difficulty level, the size of a
strafing target decreases forcing you to be more accurate.

Green Troops
target size

Elite Troops
target size

Targets for Strafing

Your cannon is effective against most ground targets. Only
very hard targets such as bunkers, or very large targets such as
runways, buildings, and bridges, cannot be destroyed with
your cannon.

Depots are especially good strafing targets, as they're
often located away from other targets and they don't shoot
back. Oil tanks also go up in a hurry under a gun attack.

Although it may be dangerous, SAM sites can make good
gun targets. If you approach from the correct angle, you can
destroy two missile launchers as well as the radar in one pass.
Once over the site you're pretty safe, as the SAM launchers
cannot shoot straight up.

Figure 4-3. SAM Radar Sites

SAM radar site
and missile
launchers.

If you plan ahead, and
are a pretty good shot,
you can take out two
launchers and the SAM
radar site all in one pass.

Weapons Selection

Choosing the right weapon for the right job is very important
if you're to have a successful mission. Most targets can be destroyed by a number of different weapons; you should choose
the one that can be delivered with the least deviation from a
good stealth profile.

The AGM-65D Maverick is by far the most versatile
weapon in your inventory. You should choose these whenever
possible. They can be delivered from 500 feet and have the
best "standoff" capability. They're extremely accurate from 16
km and reasonably accurate from 36 km.

This "standoff" ability allows you to pop up, launch the
weapon, turn away from the target, and regain a good stealth
profile all before the weapon hits the target and alerts the enemy to your presence. Unless you have a particular target in
mind, such as a runway or sub pen (military jargon for a sub

base), always fill any unused bay with Mavericks whenever they're available.

We all hate to see it, but sooner or later a mission will come up with no Mavericks available. Laser guided bombs are the next best thing. Toss bombing is easy, and the laser guidance system makes them as accurate as the Maverick. The downside is you'll have to get much closer to your target to drop them.

Some targets require a specific ordnance. Use Durandals to destroy runways. CBU-72 FAE bombs should be used against sub pens. Most other targets are vulnerable to several kinds of weapons. Again, don't forget about your cannon.

Plan Your Attack

The time to make your battle plan is during the briefing portion of the game. Here you have all of the intelligence information you'll need. Once in the air, it's too late. Sure, things will happen in the heat of battle that may disrupt even the best plans, but it's much better to have a plan and change it than to have no plan at all.

Just because the waypoints are set a certain way doesn't mean this is the best path to take. Sometimes it might be safer to pass the secondary target and attack the primary target first. Even though the secondary target might be closer, if you hit it first the area could be full of MiGs by the time you get to the primary target. You can always hit a secondary target like this one on the way home.

You should look at the radar coverage and pick the safest path. Sometimes this might take you out of your way. This is often the case when flying in the North Cape area. Targets along the coast can best be approached by flying way out to sea, out of radar coverage, and then zipping straight in to attack the targets. You can head back home via the same route. And if you come up short of fuel, you can always put down on the USS *Kennedy*, which is usually in a convenient position.

Good planning leads to more points. A good case in point is how you plan your entry and egress. When heading into enemy territory, the longer you can go unnoticed, the better. This

61

might mean flying right past a fat target or letting a MiG pass right through your gunsights. Anytime you attack a target, the enemy is alerted and a herd of aircraft will be vectored in your direction. Also, try to stay away from enemy air bases.

Reaction time for enemy aircraft is largely based on your distance from the nearest base. Make them use up a lot of fuel and time if they come after you. You want the enemy to be totally unaware of your presence until that prized primary or secondary target goes up in flames. Also, plan to pick up extra targets on the way home. Those missile boats you avoided on the way in can be hit on the way out if you plan ahead. These boats are great for strafing practice.

Use Standoff When Attacking Multiple Targets

If you're going to use Mavericks to attack two targets that are close together, pick an approach path that will maximize your standoff capability on both targets. If you attack them in a straight line, you'll have to fly right over the first target to get to the second. And since enemy aircraft will start heading for the first target as soon as it's hit, it may get rather crowded. You're better off to fly parallel to the targets at a good standoff range and make quick turns toward the targets to lock and fire your weapon.

On the other hand, if you're going to drop a bomb on one target and use a Maverick on the other, it would be better to approach them in line. Use your standoff advantage on the second target. In this case you should align the targets so the one to be bombed is first in line. This way, you can drop your bomb on the first target and fire the Maverick at the second target at the same time. Then you're free to turn away and leave the area before the bad guys show up.

Figure 4-4. Use Maximum Standoff

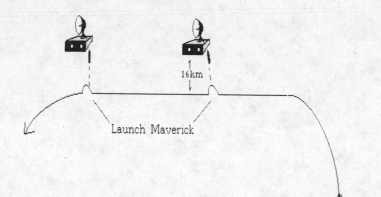

Go Around Instead of Over Hills

Although it might take you out of your way, going around hills and mountains is much safer for two reasons. First, some of the mountains are several thousand feet high. As you come over the crest you make an excellent radar target. By the time you can get back down to a safe level, you'll probably have several SAMs after you. ·

The second reason is that as you come around a mountain, you can deal with one target at a time. If you go over the crest of the hill, all of the targets on the other side will appear at the same time, much faster than you can deal with them. But as you swing around the base of the hill, the targets will come into your field of view one at a time.

Figure 4-5. Go Around Hills

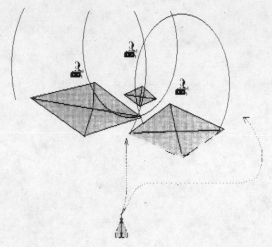

If you fly straight over these hills, you will be sighted by all three
radar sites. If you go around, you can deal with them one at a time.

Photo Reconn Missions

Although these photo reconnaissance missions are probably
not on the top of anyone's list of favorites, they're a very real
simulation of how a Stealth Fighter would actually be used. In
fact, since the aircraft has been in operation for the past five
years, I think it safe to assume this type of mission has already
taken place.

Using the camera isn't that difficult, but there are a few
things you need to keep in mind. Once the camera is selected,
the tracking camera that produces the lower right-hand screen
is locked into a fixed position so it can act as the viewer for
the reconn camera in the bay. You need to approach the target
low—200 feet is good. When you're about 4 km away, open

the bay doors and get ready to shoot. Even though you're given the small box on the HUD to aim with, it's more important to make sure the target appears on the lower right-hand screen. Use this screen as your aiming guide. Snap the picture when the target is on this screen, and you should get a good shot. Also, don't be afraid to try a number of shots as you approach the target; I've never run out of film on a photo run.

A nice steady run is the key here. If you detect a SAM launch or have MiG problems, use your decoys or ECM until you finish the run. You just can't fight and shoot photos at the same time. But do take the necessary precautions to make sure you survive. Remember, a photo mission isn't successful unless you land safely to deliver the film; bailing out just won't cut it.

Check Both Map Displays Often

Sometimes in the heat of battle, especially if you get hit, your onboard computer may get a little scrambled and mess up your waypoint settings. If you blindly follow the NAV cursor on the HUD without occasionally checking your location on the map, you may be heading in a totally wrong direction. For this reason it's important to frequently check the *Satellite Map* as well as the *Tactical Display*. Always double check both displays after you take a hit.

If your waypoints do get scrambled, your primary and secondary targets show up on the Satellite Map as flashing dots. You can find them easily by flying in their general direction and locating them with the TrackCam.

A Few Defensive Suggestions

In all cases, your best defense is to remain unseen. This is why we spent so much money to develop the Stealth Fighter in the first place.

Although there are numerous types of ground-based radar systems, there are really only two broad categories, *pulse* and *doppler* types. It's important to know what type of radar you're up against and react accordingly. If you haven't made a note of it beforehand, you can go to the Satellite Map to find out the type of an enemy radar. Dotted lines radiating from a radar source indicate a pulse radar. Solid lines indicate a doppler system.

The manual does a very good job explaining how to avoid detection by both types of radar; you should reread that section several times. Here's a summary of the techniques. Pulse type radars can best be fooled by flying straight at them and then turning away quickly between pulses. You should start to notice the time interval between radar pulses as you approach a radar site. Remember, the lower and slower you go, the harder you'll be to detect. Once you're as close as you can get, wait for a pulse; then immediately turn hard away from the site. You must act quickly and finish your turn with your wings once again level before the next pulse.

Doppler types are very different. They work best against targets that come directly at them or directly away from them. You should approach these cautiously; once you're as close as you can safely get, you can get past them by maintaining a constant distance from the site as you swing around its arc.

Sometimes, despite your best efforts, you're going to be seen and the TRACK indicator will start to flash. What do you do? Well, the first thing you should NOT do is turn and run at high speed. The F-19 wasn't designed to outrun anyone. You need to use your strongest weapon, which is stealth. Try to break the lock by disappearing. Reduce your speed if you can and fly a little lower. Hide behind a hill or mountain if one is close by. Do whatever it takes to break the radar lock.

But sometimes you just can't. In this case you need to take out the radar that spotted you. Even if there are a half dozen MiGs buzzing around you, chances are they're getting their information from one ground-based radar or an IL-76 AWACS plane. Destroy the one site that has a lock on you, and the rest will be blind. This is why it's very important to keep an eye on all radar sites that are getting close to detection. Knowing which one has a lock on you is very important.

Don't let stray SAM shots spook you. Sometimes when the enemy knows you're out there somewhere but can't find you, they'll shoot a SAM in your general direction trying to panic you into showing yourself. If you react by dropping chaff or turning on your jammers, they'll lock onto you for sure. Unless the TRACK indicator on your panel is lit, they don't know where you are. If the SAM is heading straight for you, it might be just a lucky shot. A small course change may be all that's necessary to get out of its way.

The one exception is handheld SAMs that are fired at you when you wander over a heavy troop concentration. These short-range SAMs aren't very dangerous unless they lock onto you. In this case, a few flares and a course change should defeat them. Don't just drop a flare and continue on your way. If the missile loses you, it will continue on its last course. If you stay on the same heading, it may hit you anyway. The best way to avoid this problem is to note the locations of troop concentrations during the Special Activities portion of the preflight briefing. If you stay away from these locations, you won't have to deal with the problem.

Chapter 5
Air-to-Air Tactics

5
Air-to-Air Tactics

One look at the F-19 and it's pretty obvious it wasn't designed with the air-to-air role in mind. It's heavy, slow, and underpowered. But its stealth characteristics do offer it the unique advantage of almost always being able to get off the first shot. This advantage shouldn't be overlooked, as from World War I all the way through Vietnam and the Falkland Islands, most successful air attacks came as a total surprise to the victims. They never knew what hit them.

This is the attitude you need to take when getting involved in air combat with F-19. You must make the first shot count. Your strongest weapon is stealth; use it wisely. You can go one of two ways with this strategy. Either engage your enemy at long range, firing a missile and then disappearing, or sneak up so close that you can't miss. Either way is okay; it's the situations in between that will get you in trouble. The F-19 isn't very maneuverable, so you'll have a hard time out-turning a clever opponent. It's also not very fast, so you won't be able to outrun anyone.

Once engaged, you have only two options: Either destroy the enemy aircraft or use your stealth capability to disappear until the situation improves. In a one-on-one encounter, either is fairly simple. But many encounters in F-19 are against multiple aircraft, sometimes four or more. Here's where knowing how to use all of your weapons and superior tactics really pays dividends.

Missile Shots

With a normal fighter, the first part of an air combat engagement is a missile exchange. Though this isn't necessarily the case with the F-19, we'll cover it first anyway.

When the targeting box first changes to an oval, you're at the maximum range for that missile. That maximum range is calculated assuming you're at maximum speed to give the missile that extra boost. In many situations, you'll be flying at very low speed when you wish to fire a missile. In these cases, you should wait until the oval changes color before firing. In fact, the increase in accuracy after the oval changes color is so great, you should almost always wait for the change. The Highly Effective range for Sidewinders is inside of 9 km; for AMRAAMs it's inside of 16 km.

The one exception to the rule is when shooting at a target that's coming at you head-on. If you wait until the oval turns red for a head-on shot, the range will likely be so short that the missile will fly past the target before it has a good chance to lock on. In these situations, a shot at close to maximum range is a good idea. This will give the missile plenty of time to acquire the target and maneuver for a hit. The target will likely be in the Highly Effective range by the time the weapon arrives.

Figure 5-1. Head-On Missile Shot

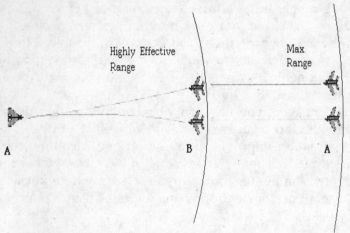

Highly Effective Range

Max. Range

A   B   A

Since the bogeys are coming at the attacker head-on, the attacker can fire missiles at position A (max range). By the time the missiles reach the targets, the bogeys will have moved into the more effective range.

Head-on shots can be a very good tactic against multiple bogeys. You can fire AMRAAMs from close to the maximum range of 35 km at each target and then disappear to watch the results. If you haven't been detected, you can then maneuver for short-range gun or sidewinder shots at the survivors.

Both Sidewinders and AMRAAMs are all-aspect missiles. That is, they can track a target at any angle. But I prefer to use AMRAAMs for long-range head-on shots and save the side-winders for rear quarter, tailpipe shots. Unfortunately, neither is always effective, especially against Veteran and Elite level pilots.

For missile shots to be effective against these high-level opponents, range is the key. You must get in close. Long shots give them plenty of time to react and avoid the missile. However, a long shot, to keep them busy while you close in for a shorter shot, can be effective.

Gun Attacks

Missiles are great, but there are times when nothing but the gun will do. A U.S. Navy gunnery instructor once said, "There's no kill like a guns kill." He knew what he was talking about. A guns battle is one of the few times in this age of faceless, long-range warfare where you get close enough to you opponent to get a good look at him. When you're close enough for a guns engagement, you can actually see the enemy aircraft well. His twists and turns are easy to see and follow.

The Historical Gunsight

Gunsights have come a long way over the years. They've advanced from a circle and crosshairs mounted in front of the wind screen, to complex, computer-driven devices that make all sorts of calculations for the pilot. The "historical" or real-time sight is the most accurate type of sight yet developed. This type of sight displays where the cannon shells would impact if they were fired roughly two seconds ago. I'm often asked why the sight doesn't show where the shells will be two seconds FROM NOW. Well, this type of "predicting" sight was developed and used, but it requires a great deal of predicting. If both the target and the shooter are maneuvering wildly, this predicting becomes very questionable. The historical gunsight allows for all kinds of maneuvering since it uses known, not predicted information. The computer knows where you and the target were two seconds ago and can show an extremely accurate picture of where shells fired then would have hit.

Using this type of sight does take a little getting used to. You must base your aim on where the aiming pipper will be in two seconds or so. This will be shorter if you're very close to the target. Rather than looking at where the pipper is, you need to concentrate on which direction it's moving relative to the target. You need to time your shot so the pipper will reach the target in two seconds or so.

This sounds difficult in concept, but it's much easier to learn than it is to explain. Pilots prefer this type of sight to all others because it gives them very accurate information. With good information, they know they can aim the system properly. With a little practice, I'm sure you'll be able to master the system. Once you do, watch out MiGs!

Pursuit Curves

There are three kinds of pursuit curves: *lag, pure,* and *lead.*
Most people instinctively use *pure pursuit*—they point the
nose of their planes directly at the bad guys. This approach is
okay, but lead and lag pursuit offer distinct advantages in *F-19
Stealth Fighter.* The most important one to know about in *F-19*
is *lead pursuit.* Pursuit curves describe the course you take as
you follow a target. This generally means where you point the
nose of the aircraft. Following a lead pursuit curve, keeping
your nose ahead of the bad guy assures that you can "pull
lead" on the target for a good guns shot.

Here's why "pulling lead" is so important. If you're in a
turning fight with another aircraft and you have your nose
pointed directly at him, despite what you may think, he's perfectly safe. You see, it takes a certain amount of time for the
shells you fire to travel the distance between you and the target. By the time the shells get there, the target will be gone.
It's just like throwing a football to a running receiver. You
don't throw it to where he is but where he'll be by the time
the ball gets there. The same thing applies to gunnery. You
must shoot where the target will be, not where it is.

Figure 5-2. Pure Pursuit

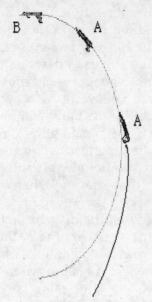

This illustration shows why Pure Pursuit will not work in a gun battle. At position A the attacker has his nose pointed directly at the bogey. But if he fires, the bogey will move to position B before the shells arrive, causing a miss.

Figure 5-3. Lead Pursuit

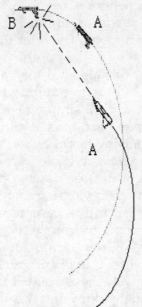

By taking a Lead Pursuit curve and pointing his nose AHEAD of the bogey at position A, the attacker is able to "pull lead" and aim his cannon shells in front of the target so that the shells and the target both arrive at position B simultaneously.

When you're following a target in a lead-pursuit curve, you have lead on that target. In other words, your nose is pointing in front of the target, not at it. This allows you to shoot where the target will be, not where it is. If you get into an engagement using lead pursuit from the beginning, you won't have to outturn your opponent. Rather than flying straight at him, use the Tactical display or the TrackCam to see which way he is heading or turning, and then approach with your nose pointed in front of him, not at him. Be careful not to lead the target too much or he'll simply reverse his course and put you on the defensive. Lead pursuit will also allow you to close range on a faster moving target by letting you "take a shortcut" and cut across the turning circle.

Lag-pursuit, or keeping your nose pointed behind the target, can be effectively used when you're trying to track a maneuvering target from the rear. In this case, trying to pull lead on the target will only get you into trouble. What generally happens is as you pull hard on the turn to get your nose ahead of the target, he reverses course and catches you going the wrong way. By keeping your nose pointed behind the target, he'll have to pass through your gunsights if he reverses course, giving you the chance for a quick guns shot. By maintaining a lag-pursuit position you'll also be able to maintain a speed advantage over the enemy. If he does not reverse, you may be able to force him into an ever-tightening turn. Sooner or later he will run out of airspeed or altitude and be forced to make a straight line run for it. Then you can use your speed advantage to close for a gun shot or to line him up for a missile.

Lateral Separation

Use lateral separation combined with lead pursuit to attack those unsuspecting targets. Putting a little space between your flightpath and the bogey's will make your turn and attack much easier. That way you won't have to turn and race after him; you'll be able to keep your nose in front of the target the whole time. You can either maintain the lead pursuit until you close the range for a gun shot or slide in behind him and put a Sidewinder up his tailpipe.

Figure 5-4. Lateral Separation

The Low Speed Yo-Yo

Since the F-19 spends so much of its time at very low speed and low altitude, many of the classic fighter maneuvers don't translate well. They assume a different kind of fight. One that does work very well, however, is the *Low Speed Yo-Yo*. There are a number of Yo-Yo maneuvers named after a Chinese fighter pilot who used them in the Korean war. They generally involve maneuvering up or down to decrease or increase airspeed.

The situation for a Low Speed Yo-Yo is when you're in a hard turning fight and cannot out-turn your opponent to pull lead for a gun shot. Since you need to keep the nose up in most hard turns with the F-19, you tend to gain altitude in the process. This Yo-Yo maneuver lets you trade some of that altitude for speed and cut across the turning circle to gain an advantage over the enemy.

To describe the maneuver, let's assume you're in the following situation. You're in a hard turning fight, banking sharply, chasing the tail of an opponent turning in the same direction. To perform the Yo-Yo maneuver you should:

1. Continue to roll over so you're slightly inverted and pull your nose down so you start an inverted dive. (Note that you're not totally inverted, just a little past a 90-degree bank.) As you roll over, you should momentarily get a stall warning indication. Once you get inverted, it should stop— don't worry about it.
2. Pull back hard on the stick as you dive to make your turn tighter. The speed you pick up in the dive should keep you from stalling.
3. You should only stay in this diving turn for a second or two before you roll back over in the opposite direction and pull out of the dive. If you've performed the maneuver well, you should have made up a lot of ground on the bogey.

Figure 5-5. Low Speed Yo-Yo

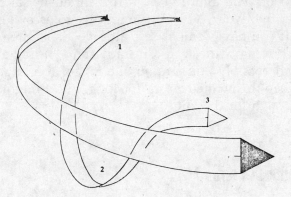

Roll down inside the other aircraft's turn, then pull up for a possible shot.

The Straight Yo-Yo

A similar maneuver can be used to close the range on planes flying away from you. Since most, if not all, enemy aircraft can fly faster than your F-19, they might try to escape by running away. If you have some excess altitude, as is often the case after a turning battle, you can trade some of that altitude for speed and possibly pull into missile range. You might not be able to keep this maneuver up for long, but it might get you close enough for the kill.

Figure 5-6. Straight Yo-Yo

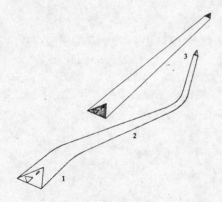

Trade altitude for airspeed by making a shallow dive. If you get close enough, pull up for a gun shot or to get the bogey into the missile envelope.

The Forced Overshoot

Enemy pilots seem to have an uncanny ability to know what you're doing almost immediately. This technique uses that against them. If you have a bogey that you just can't shake, you might want to try this somewhat risky maneuver. Let the bogey come around on your tail, but be ready to jink a missile or two. Slow up so you draw him in real close; then go to max power. He'll react almost instantly with max power, too. When he starts to overtake you, cut the engines and put out the brake to force him to overshoot. Almost always, he'll pass above you and turn quickly, usually to the left. Be ready to pull the nose up and shoot as soon as he appears.

Multiple Bogeys

The presence of more than one enemy aircraft presents a whole new set of problems. Now you can't concentrate on one bogey too long or the other will sneak around behind you and let you have it. The enemy has a good deal of intelligence in this game. They frequently place fighter patrols in gaps in radar coverage. Sometimes you have no alternative but to take on two or more fighters. If there's no way to avoid the fight, it's much better to be on the offensive.

Take the fight to the enemy at the first possible moment. Long-range missile shots may be successful and eliminate the need for further battle, or at least even the odds some. If you have several bogeys approaching from different angles, try to take out the most dangerous one first. Or if only one has radar lock on you, go after him first and then hide from the rest until you can plan your attack. Remember, in most cases, especially at night, you can simply disappear.

Also remember, just because two aircraft are heading right for you doesn't mean they have a good fix on your position or even know you're there. Aircraft will always head to the site of the most recent action. So even though it might appear as if they're headed for you, they could be just responding to your latest attack.

Fake Attacks

If you're closing in on an important target with a lot of air cover, it's much easier to lure the enemy aircraft away than it is to try and fight them and attack a ground target at the same time. A good way to do this is to attack something that's 90 degrees off of your flight path. Use as much standoff as possible. A Maverick shot off to the side from 35 km is perfect for this task. If you get low and slow, and then head away from the fake attack site, the enemy air cover will pass right by you, letting you continue to the primary target area unopposed. Be aware that once you attack that target, they'll all head back to you in a hurry. If you don't want to use one of your Mavericks, you can pop up, let yourself be seen on radar by opening your bay doors and so on, and then disappear again to low altitude. This will draw the enemy aircraft to your last known position; if you move away in a hurry, you can avoid them. Doing it this way, however, doesn't give you the extra 35 km the Maverick attack does.

Air-to-Air Missions

Air-to-air missions aren't the real purpose for the Stealth Fighter, so you generally get fewer points for them. But they are a lot of fun. One problem often seen by players is that of finding the Primary target. Ground targets are easy—they don't move. But air targets move so fast they're sometimes hard to find.

One frequent air-to-air mission target is a AN-72 Coaler Transport. At first these are a little hard to find; your tactical might may show a half dozen aircraft in the air, but which is the AN-72? There's an easy way to tell: Just look for an aircraft that's not putting out a radar signal. That's probably it. If your target is an IL-76, just look for an aircraft putting out a huge signal.

Another critical thing you need to know about air-to-air missions is they'll often reroute the target plane if there's even a hint of trouble in the area. This is especially true if the plane is carrying important supplies or high-ranking officials. So keep this in mind and don't make too much noise on the way in. This goes for flying over enemy positions as well. Even if you aren't picked up on radar, you might be seen or heard and reported. If this happens, your target might turn and head back home or to another base, landing before you can get there.

You should also be aware that many of the air-to-air missions have an unwritten time limit. If you're to intercept a plane traveling from point A to point B, you must get him before he reaches point B. Once he arrives at his destination, he'll circle the airfield once or twice and land. Once he lands, your chances of completing your mission are gone. There are a couple of points here in your favor, though. If the main target is traveling with a fighter escort, one or two of the fighters might land first, giving you a couple of extra seconds. If you see the message that the target is on final, your only hope is to try a long-range shot. This will occasionally spook them enough to cause them to break off the landing pattern to take evasive action.

Landing Enemy Planes

Be aware that once you get that message on the HUD saying a plane is on final approach to an airbase, it's locked into landing and very vulnerable. It might be too far away to worry about, but if it's close by, it's easy cannon fodder—especially those big IL-76s.

Decoys

The three decoys you carry aren't only good against enemy SAMs, they'll also fool enemy aircraft. This can come in real handy if you're surrounded by several MiGs that all have a good radar lock on you. Just pop a decoy and try to disappear before it expires. Or use the time to gain a good firing position while they chase the decoy. You might be able to take out two or three during the confusion.

Use Your Flaps

Your flaps increase your lift and decrease your stall speed, not only during takeoff and landing, but during dogfights as well. Extending your flaps will decrease your stall speed in a hard turn from 250 knots to 210 knots. This will let you hold a turn a little longer and might give you the edge you need.

Chapter 6
Tips and Hints for Playing the Commodore 64 Version of *Project Stealth Fighter*

6
Tips and Hints for Playing the Commodore 64 Version of *Project Stealth Fighter*

About a year or so before the IBM version of *F-19* was released, MicroProse shipped *Project Stealth Fighter* for the Commodore 64/128. This game is really the father of *F-19*. And like father and son, the two games are similar in appearance but quite different upon closer inspection. The game sold quite well on the Commodore platform, so even though this book is mainly about the IBM version, I didn't want to leave out the C64 fans.

This chapter includes tips and hints, as well as scoring, promotion, and medal awards information that mainly applies to the C64 version ONLY. Related information pertaining to the IBM version can be found elsewhere in the book.

So for those of you still playing the Commodore version, this chapter is for you. The rest of you with the IBM version might want to read through it anyway if you're interested in the history of *F-19 Stealth Fighter*.

The Big Hint

If you only remember one hint from this chapter, remember this one: Maintaining a low stealth profile is very important, for a number of reasons. It improves your Stealth Rating and your score, and it reduces the chances of your being spotted by enemy radar. The best way to keep a low profile is to fly low and slow. Flight below 500 feet, where your profile is the lowest, however, can be very difficult. Constant altitude adjustments are necessary to keep from hitting the ground or popping up to 1000 feet.

Flight below 500 feet can be difficult—that is, unless you know the trick: There's a combination of pitch and airspeed that will allow you to fly hands-off at altitudes below 500 feet. This point will be different for each weapon's load and fuel level, but it's generally in the area of nine degrees of pitch and 250–275 knots.

The best way to find this combination is to fly at 900 feet and then set the pitch to nine degrees; this is indicated in the lower portion of the HUD (Heads-Up Display). Now decrease the throttle. Watch the Vertical Velocity Indicator bar gauge; when it indicates a slight descent, you're almost there. Now let the plane descend to below 500 feet. This should be a very slow descent; if not, increase your throttle by one notch. Once below 500 feet, you should have only one blue light showing on your EMV (Electro-Magnetic Visibility) bar. Increase throttle by one notch. This should stop your descent and leave you in level flight at 400 feet or so. Now if you want to change altitude you can increase or reduce throttle. If you can't fly steadily at this point and you reach a situation where one notch more of throttle causes the plane to rise while one notch less causes it to sink, adjust the pitch one notch up or down and repeat your throttle adjustment. This process becomes second nature with a little practice.

Once you master the technique of finding this smooth-flying slot, you'll be able to greatly increase your stealth percentage by flying consistently below 500 feet. Remember that you burn fuel faster at this altitude, so it might not be right for all missions. Also, be careful when flying in this manner near mountains, as the erratic winds near them will move you out of the slot and cause you to rise or sink. If you sink to 300 feet, there won't be a lot of air under you.

Radar Ranges

There's a drawing on page 42 of the manual that shows how to draw circles around all enemy positions to see the range of the radar at each installation. This would help you thread the needle, allowing you to plan your path just outside of radar range and thus minimizing your exposure. It isn't very clear how to do that, however, so I'll try and explain it.

Turn to page 64 in the manual. You'll see a SAM chart, and under the heading "Max Range for Search" there's a number in parentheses. This number shows the radar range in numbers of blocks on the maps provided. If you knew a SAM location had SA-2 missiles, you could go to the chart and find that the range was three. You could then use a compass to measure three blocks and draw a circle around the SAM site indicating the range of the radar. If you do this for all the radar installations in the area, you'll be able to visualize the best route through them.

HARMs and Harpoons

Both HARM (High-speed Anti-Radiation Missile) and Harpoon missiles are excellent for accomplishing specific missions: blasting radar and ships. The problem with these missiles is that you're limited to one missile in each weapons bay.

To earn a high score, you'll need to hit extra ground targets, but carrying one missile in each bay limits that ability. A good solution is to carry the multipurpose Maverick missile. The Maverick has a better range than the HARM and is just as effective. It does have a shorter range than the Harpoon, but you can safely get within Maverick range of most ships with little problem. The main benefit of the Maverick is you can carry two missiles in each bay. This allows you an extra missile for those important extra ground targets.

Weapons Are Internal

Remember that all the weapons carried by the F-19 are carried internally. When you activate these weapons and open the bay doors, you increase drag and reduce lift. Get into the habit of increasing the throttle just before you activate your weapons. Doing so will prevent finding out the hard way you're losing altitude.

This applies to dogfighting as well as to air-to-ground situations. If you're trying to out-turn a MiG, you're better off closing the bay doors until you're close to firing position. By doing so you'll increase the turning performance of your aircraft and reduce the chances of stalling. You can use the air-to-air tracking mode to keep track of the enemy while keeping the doors shut; use the Switch Tracking Mode key to activate it.

Panic Shots

The enemy will often take shots with SAMs and AAMs (Air-to-Air Missiles) that don't have a chance of hitting you; they're just trying to trick you into using your ECM (Electronic CounterMeasures) systems and giving away your location. When you're entering or leaving an area with a good stealth profile, go to the 12-mile radar screen if fired upon. Many times the missile won't even come within 12 miles of you, and if it does, its lock may be too weak to hit you. Wait until the last second before using ECM, and use jammers only briefly. This will minimize your exposure.

Runway Landings

A common problem for beginning players is lining up the jet for runway landings. Most give up too soon. They come in low on fuel and have trouble getting properly lined up. When they give up and try to go around again, they run out of fuel.

You don't have to start your landing at the very end of the runway. The runways are very long and wide, so you can be way out of line as you go over the start of the strip and still have time to straighten up and land on the last third of the runway. You'll be flying very slowly, so you have more time than you think. You'll be surprised at how fast the aircraft stops rolling after touchdown once you've cut the engines and put on the brakes.

In fact, I don't recommend trying to land at the beginning of the strip; it's very hard to judge when you're over the runway and it's easy to land too short, thereby ruining an otherwise good mission. Give yourself lots of room and set your plane down gently. You have plenty of time.

Enemy AWACS

Enemy AWACS (Airborne Warning And Control System) planes can cause a lot of problems in the North Cape and Central Europe scenarios. They can see you, but you can't see them. If you've been spotted but you can't see anything on your radar, you've probably been seen by an AWACS. The AWACS plane and its escorts will circle at a specific altitude, which changes from game to game. As a rule, however, they can generally be found in the high 20s or high 30s.

It's possible to fly under AWACS coverage, but you must be very stealthy. AWACS radar, like any other radar, can be fooled if you fly low and slow enough.

A good way to take them out is to follow the "Operation Dreamland" flight plan described in Tom Clancy's book, *Red Storm Rising*. In this scenario, the F-19 pilot zips in under the AWACS coverage by staying low, and then once he's almost directly under the Il-76 he guns the engines and heads straight up to fire a missile shot. If you get an air-to-air mission where you must attack an Il-76, give it a try!

Two-Player System

In the heat of battle, everything seems to happen at once. An extra pair of eyes and hands can be a big help. Many players have commented they consistently score higher when they play with another experienced player at the keyboard. The following is one way to divide the responsibilities.

Pilot Responsibilities:

• Fly the aircraft.
• Set the course.
• Fire the weapons.
• Give the orders.

Copilot Responsibilities:

• Change the radar display scale.
• Activate the ECM and decoys.
• Activate and select weapons.
• Keep an eye on the altitude during bomb runs and dogfights.
• Check all systems for damage after an enemy hit.
• ID and switch targets.
• Change map displays.

Since the copilot isn't involved with flying the plane, he or she can be given more duties to keep occupied.

Extra Fuel

Fuel is a critical item. You have to get to the target, destroy it, destroy extra ground or air targets, and return home. You'll rarely find this possible on the minimum amount listed as you arm your plane. If a mission has a minimum fuel amount of 9,900 pounds, you should think seriously about leaving some weapons behind and taking more fuel instead. Even then you'll have to be frugal: The extra tanks don't carry very much. Be conservative with your throttle and altitude.

There are a couple of things you need to know about the Extra Fuel. You can activate the fuel as soon as you take off. Doing so has the odd effect of increasing your speed and thus your range. The fuel is still there to use, but the computer no longer takes the extra weight into consideration when calculating the fuel consumption rate. If you think you'll have to glide most of the way home from your mission, you might want to wait before using the extra fuel. Go ahead and let the aircraft run out of fuel (make sure any extra weapons are dropped) and start your glide. Now activate the extra fuel but don't start your engines yet. When you're close to the base, you can restart the engines and use the extra fuel for your landing maneuvers.

Gliding

Under certain circumstances, if you don't turn or maneuver, you should be able to glide almost indefinitely. It glides best when the weapons bays are empty. By pitching the nose up to around nine degrees you'll be just above stall speed, and you should be able to get the Vertical Velocity Indicator to level out. This maneuver won't work if you have a lot of fuel left, due to the added weight.

Fuel Efficiency

The aircraft fuel consumption rate goes down as you increase in altitude, up to 32,000 feet. This is shown in an increase in airspeed for a particular throttle setting. The effect of this increase in airspeed is an increase in range.

Additional Ground Targets

Additional ground targets are essential for high scores. Although from a scoring standpoint all ground targets count the same, destroying certain targets will be more beneficial to you than others. Also, some weapons are more effective on certain targets than others.

If you have light weapons, SAM radar sites are excellent targets. Destroying a site will disable all of the launchers. These can be easily strafed if you have the time. It's often a good idea to take out a nearby SAM radar first before attacking the major objective.

If you have some heavy weapons left, take out a runway. Enemy planes will scramble from the closest runway. If the nearest runway is destroyed, they'll have to come from the next closest base, which might be very distant. This should make your flight home a lot easier!

Enemy Fighters

Each type of enemy plane is programmed with different capabilities, as is each type of air-to-air missile. But the airplane and missile attributes don't have as large an effect on the dogfighting capability as the quality of the enemy pilot. Green pilots will generally fly cautiously, keeping their planes flat and attempting few aerobatics. Average pilots will be somewhat more aggressive. Veteran pilots will use a variety of vertical maneuvers you won't be able to duplicate. Engaging a Veteran enemy pilot in a dogfight isn't advised. Even the folks at MicroProse have a hard time with them. You'd be better off dealing with them at long range and then using stealth to escape.

The good news about enemy fighters is they can use only missiles against you. They aren't programmed for cannon attacks.

Also, it's to your advantage that enemy fighters are vectored to your last known position instead of on an intercept course with your heading. They can be "faked out" if you let yourself be seen a distance from your target area. Once you're seen, the fighters will head for your current position. If you're not there when they arrive and you haven't been sighted elsewhere, they'll hang around for a few minutes and then go home. So if you can get a low stealth profile, you can fly on toward your target without problems from enemy fighters.

Strafing Attacks

One great way to increase your scores is to master the art of strafing targets. You carry all that cannon ammunition, so you might as well learn to use it. You must be below 500 feet for a successful attack, and your range is only 2.5 miles. Flying very slowly is the key. The manual recommends using the speed brake, but it's easier to use your flaps to increase lift and decrease stall speed. Line the target up and dip the nose slightly as you fire. Keep an eye on your altitude; making smoking holes in the ground won't win any medals.

Most targets will take several strafing hits to destroy. Some (runways, for instance) are almost impossible to destroy with your gun. On the other hand, oil tanks go up nicely under gunfire.

Organize Your Weapons Bay

If you take the time to organize your weapons before you take off, you can save precious seconds in the heat of battle. Some people like to put all air-to-air missiles in the top two bays and air-to-ground weapons in the bottom bays. I generally put the weapon I'm going to use on the Primary Target in Bay 1, and if I'm carrying extra fuel I'll put it in Bay 4. Organize them any way you like, but keep things the same so you'll know where they are at all times. You don't have time to pull up the weapons inventory in the middle of a dogfight.

Scoring System

As with all MicroProse games, the scoring system for *Stealth Fighter* is complicated. MicroProse tried to take into account all of the various options.

First you have a score based on the values of all the targets destroyed. That number is then multiplied by a factor value. This factor value is based on

- Region
- Tension
- Mission
- Range
- Enemy quality
- Realism
- Landing

Depending upon your choices for these items, the factor value may be larger or smaller than 1, thereby increasing or decreasing your basic score. If all options are at their hardest levels, your basic score can be increased by a factor of 9.

The following describes all items that go into making the factor value. In order of importance, they are

1. Region
2. Tension, enemy quality, and realism
3. Range
4. Mission type

Landing safely at a base will keep your score the same. Bailing out over the deep ocean costs you a few points, bailing out over friendly territory costs more, and bailing out over enemy territory (including coastal waters) will cost you heavily.

Let's examine each of the categories.

Region. Western Europe provides the most points. The North Cape provides only slightly less. These are followed by the Persian Gulf, Libya, and training.

Tension. In order of importance from highest tension to lowest, the levels of tension are Conventional War, Limited War, and Cold War.

Enemy Quality. The enemy may be a Veteran flier, a Regular, or Green (inexperienced).

Realism. The quality of realism will be either Realistic Flight, Easy Flight, or No Crash.

Range. The range is based on the Fuel Distance Estimate provided at the beginning of the mission. The range falls into one of four categories: 11,500 or more; 9,000 to 11,499; 7,000 to 8,999; and 6,999 or less.

Mission Type. There are also four levels of mission types: Ground Target, Aircraft Target, Air-to-Air Practice, and Bombing Practice.

Promotions

Promotions are based on three things: number of missions flown, total score, and average score per mission. The average score prevents bad players from being promoted simply by flying a large number of missions.

To give some idea of the promotion process, MicroProse provided the following information. The numbers might not be exact, but you should get some idea of the process.

Table 6-1. Factors Affecting Promotions

Rank	Number of Missions	Total Score	Average Score
First Lieutenant	2	400	150
Captain	5	1500	200
Major	10	3300	230
Lieutenant Colonel	20	7250	260
Full Colonel	40	16000	280
Brigadier General	99	22000	220

As you can see, it's important to keep your average score up. Don't record low-scoring missions. Also note you must meet all of the criteria to be promoted. If you fly enough missions and achieve the required total score but your average is below par, you still won't be promoted.

Medals

Winning a medal is based solely on your performance on a particular mission; no other items are taken into account. Your score for that mission is the determining factor.

The values shown for earning medals might not be exact, but they should be in the ball park. The one-mission score values are shown below.

Table 6-2. One-Mission Score Values

Medal	Score
Congressional Medal of Honor	1800
Distinguished Flying Cross	1300
Silver Star	850
Bronze Star	500
Airman's Medal	250

To win a second medal of any type, you must score a little more than twice the original total. In other words, you'll win your first Silver Star before you win a second Bronze Star, and so on. To win your Third of any medal type requires more than three times the original total. This keeps you from racking up 20 or 30 Airman's Medals without improving your flying.

Chapter 7
Scoring, Promotions, and Decorations

7
Scoring, Promotions, and Decorations

I've heard some people asked why they bother with scoring, promotions, and the rest of it. Why not just concentrate on the simulation and forget the rest? Therein lies the difference between simulations and simulation games. Most people like to have an objective way to rate their performances. Other than having someone else grade them over their shoulders as they play, some sort of scoring system is the only way to do that. These systems allow players to rate not only each other, but the performance of various strategy ideas. With a score in hand, players can tell if their skills are improving and establish their skill levels when compared to other players.

The promotion scale serves a similar purpose of establishing a skill level, and it also says something about the players' frequency of success and how long they've been playing the game.

Decorations serve a similar purpose too, but they also perform another important function. Every game should have an ultimate goal—something that establishes players as having attained an expert level of skill. Medals do that in *F-19*. Winning the Congressional Medal of Honor is the ultimate goal of most *F-19* pilots. They also serve as a little bit of recognition for players. "Candy at the end" is how some at MicroProse refer to them. They are rewards for a job well done and encouragements to return to the game time and time again.

Since scoring, promotions, and medals are so important to most players, this chapter is dedicated to explaining these systems. Advice will also be offered on how you can maximize your scores and rack up an impressive row of ribbons and decorations.

Scoring

The scoring system used for *F-19* is certainly the most complex I've ever seen for a simulation game, ranking right up there with many of the military board-type games. The system is so complex special quality-assurance software programs had to be written just to verify its operation.

The system is similar to other MicroProse games in that it uses point totals and multipliers. The exact makeup of the equation is rather complex and doesn't need to be understood for me to explain how it works and how to increase scores.

The first thing taken into account in scoring is the type of war you select—*Cold War, Limited War,* or *Conventional War.* All game actions have a point total assigned to them; this total varies depending on the type of war and the corresponding Rules of Engagement.

Cold War

In Cold War situations, secrecy is most important. All contact with the enemy should be avoided. If you think this will limit your score, you're wrong. Cold War offers the highest points for completing both your Primary and Secondary missions, and you get points for every minute you're behind enemy lines. Believe me, they add up quickly!

The only time you should attack a target other than the primary or secondary is when you're spotted by the enemy. Generally it will take several hits from a radar to spot you, so it's better to try and disappear rather than to fight. If the enemies get a lock and fire on you, it's better to take them out. You'll lose points for being spotted, but you'll get them back if you destroy the radar that sighted you.

Points will be taken away if you shoot at anything else. Major deductions will occur if you hit a friendly or civilian target. Remember, this is peacetime. No war has been declared. But this also works in your favor, as enemy radar installations aren't on alert. This makes it much easier to slip past them.

Limited War

This opens things up a little. All enemy military targets are legal, and you're expected to destroy as much as possible. Points are added for each minute you're behind enemy lines, but at a much slower rate than in a Cold War mission. Points are taken away for hitting illegal targets, but the reductions are smaller than in Cold War. Secrecy is still important in a Limited War. Points will be deducted if you're spotted, but as before, you can get them back by destroying the radar source. Destroying civilian or friendly targets will result in points being taken away. More points are taken for destroying friendly targets since it hurts your relationship with friendly nations in the area.

Conventional War

All the stops are pulled out in Conventional War, and be ready—the enemy radar operators are alert and looking for you. Legal targets destroyed yield the most points in Conventional War, but fewer points are awarded for completing the Primary and Secondary missions. Also, you don't receive points for time spent behind enemy lines as you do in Cold War and Limited War actions. On the plus side, no points are deducted for being spotted, and civilian targets in enemy territory are now fair game.

When you hit a target, a point total for that target is assigned, depending on the type of war you're in. This point total is then modified depending on your selection of Region, Mission, Enemy, Fuel, and Landing, as well as the End Game. The more difficult the selection, the more your point total will increase. The point totals are calculated several different ways in the code, and due to rounding differences you'll frequently get two different scores for hitting the same target.

The scoring items break down as follows; the selection giving the highest point total increase is listed first, while the selection giving the lowest point total increase is listed last:

Region: Central Europe
North Cape
Persian Gulf
Libya

Mission: Strike
Air-to-air

Fuel Required: 11,500 lbs. or more
9,000–11,499 lbs.
7,000–8,900 lbs.
6,999 lbs. or less

Enemy Quality: Elite
Veteran
Regular
Green

Landing: Realistic
Easy
No Crashes

End Game: Safe Landing
Dead
Bailout Over Ocean
Bailout Over Friendly Territory
Bailout Over Neutral Territory
Bailout Over Enemy Territory
(Safe Landing and Dead keep your score
the same; all others decease your score pro-
gressively from 25% to 75%.)

Promotions

Promotions in real life come with time served as well as consistent performance; the same is true in *F-19*. You must complete a minimum number of missions to qualify for the next rank, and you must also score a minimum number of points and have a minimum overall point average. The number of missions to qualify for the next rank increases as the ranks get higher until, at the Brigadier General level, you must have 99 missions under your belt. The other point requirements are listed below.

Rank	Min Points	Min Average
2nd Lt.	0	0
1st Lt.	300	100
Captain	1125	150
Major	3000	200
Lt. Colonel	7000	250
Colonel	16,000	280
Brig. General	27,720	280

Decorations for Valor

The awarding of a medal for valor in *F-19* is solely based on the performance in a single mission. This performance is judged on the basis of your score. To win a second medal of any type you must score twice as many points, for a third medal the point total triples, and so on. If two medals have the same point total, such as the second DFC and the first Silver Star, the most prestigious decoration is awarded. The point totals required are listed below.

Airman's Medal	100
Distinguished Flying Cross	300
Silver Star	600
Air Force Cross	900
Congressional Medal of Honor	1200

Winning the CMOH

The ultimate goal of most *F-19* pilots is to eventually win the Congressional Medal of Honor. Once you understand how the scoring system works, winning the CMOH becomes a bit easier. Contrary to what most players think, the best way to win the CMOH is by flying Cold War missions. There are two reasons for this fact. First, you get the most points for completing the primary and secondary missions in Cold War. Secondly, you get a lot of points just for spending time behind enemy lines. These points are awarded several times faster than in Limited War scenarios.

You also need to select the higher levels of difficulty from the setup parameters. Use the following guidelines:

- North Cape or Central Europe should be selected as your Region.
- Choose a Strike Mission. Not only do you get more points for them, but they can be easier to complete as the targets are stationary and will always be there when you get there.
- Choose long-distance missions. The fuel estimate should be at least 9,000 pounds and preferably over 11,500 pounds. This gives two advantages: You get the highest point multiplier for Fuel Required and you must spend a lot of time behind enemy lines.
- Try and fight against at least Veteran level troops. It might be possible to win the CMOH against Regular troops, but it won't be easy.
- You can get by with Easy Landings, but Realistic would be better.
- The End Game must be a safe landing or death. Anything else will probably reduce your score too much. You *must* complete both the Primary and Secondary missions.

Keep in mind that these are guidelines. There are many combinations of selections. Some will give good results, and some will have bad results. Try to use some of the hardest selections. Winning the CMOH with *all* the selections at their minimum levels will require a lot of time behind enemy lines.

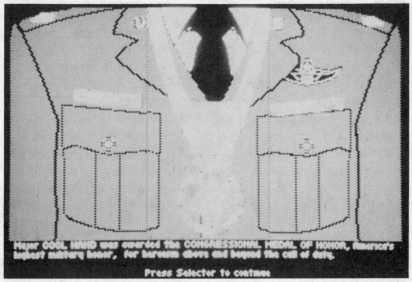

The COMH, Congressional Medal of Honor. This country's and F-19's *highest award.*

Damage

Your F-19 can take a couple of missile hits and keep flying, but something will almost always be damaged. If you've been hit, *always* take the first opportunity to check the damage display. Many times all systems seem perfectly functional, so you assume the damage was slight. This can be a deadly mistake if fuel is rapidly leaking from your tanks. A fuel leak will often cause you to cut your mission short or change your plans. If you haven't completed both missions, it might be better to continue the mission, get both targets, and then ditch in the ocean. This may yield more points than making it safely back to the base.

Two-Player System

The debate still rages as to whether the Stealth Fighter has one or two crewmembers. Since you aren't limited by space and weight, a weapons systems officer can really come in handy. When playing with two people, it's best to decide who is going to do what beforehand. One good way to divide the tasks is for one player to fly the plane, fire the weapons, and give the orders (someone has to be in charge). The other player can handle all the keyboard input and help out by keeping an eye on the instruments when the pilot is busy in combat. A second pair of eyes can be very valuable watching the altimeter and Tactical Display screens.

The Stealth Pilot Papers

I've always found it's easier to show someone how to do something than it is to tell them. That certainly holds true about computer games. A lot of ideas seem to be very abstract until you see them used in a certain situation in the context of the game. With that in mind, I set up the following pages with the idea that if you saw how some of the concepts discussed earlier were actually used, they might be easier to remember.

So strap yourself into the back seat of an F-19 and fly along with ace Stealth Fighter pilot, Captain John "the Judge" Marshall. Watch over his shoulder as he takes you on three hair-raising missions over Libya, the Persian Gulf, and the Soviet Kola Peninsula. Pay attention and you'll see how some of the concepts we saw earlier are put into practice. If you're entertained in the process, so much the better.

The Stealth Pilot Papers

OPERATION: Exterminator

OPERATION: Exterminator

The jolt of landing gear meeting runway awoke the sleeping captain. United States Air Force Captain John "the Judge" Marshall sat up blinking the sleep from his eyes and looked around the C-5B cargo plane's empty passenger area. His watch and his body were still set to California time, where it was eight in the morning. But before taking off he had set the small red hand on his watch that read military time to the correct time zone for Crete, in the Mediterranean. He looked at his watch as he stumbled into the aisle. It read 1800 hours, or six in the evening. "Geez, am I messed up."

At five feet ten inches and a stocky 180 pounds, Marshall looked like he had been stamped out of the standard mold for a fighter pilot. In the cramped john he splashed water onto his face and looked in the mirror at the three days growth of salt-and-pepper beard.

"I'm a mess."

He stuck his head into the cockpit, looking for his crew chief, who was somewhere on board.

"Last stop, Cap'n," said the C-5B pilot as he stowed his postflight checklist. The pilot worked his neck from side to side, trying to loosen the stiff muscles that always result from flying for hours with five pounds of helmet and electronics strapped to your head. "I won't say it hasn't been fun, but it hasn't been fun."

Marshall smiled, glad to see someone who looked worse than he did.

"Well, you just stick around and keep the meter running. I may be in a big hurry to get the heck outta Dodge in the morning." He clomped down the metal stairs to the cargo area, still looking for his crew chief.

"Bubba!" He shouted into the cavernous belly of the aircraft.

An impatient, "WHAT?" was the only reply. Two years of working together on the top secret Stealth Fighter project had broken down most of the formality between the officer and the enlisted man.

Below, crew chief Bubba Spencer was making the first series of checks on "his" F-19 Stealth Fighter. "Looks like she came through the flight OK, even though that blockhead bunny-hopped the landing." Actually the landing had been fine, but the Chief had yet to see a landing smooth enough for his liking. Behind the squat black F-19 sat two Palletized Work Stations, which contained everything the chief would need to work on the aircraft. He dragged a large yellow cable from the closest one and plugged it in to the belly. Turning on the Portable Power Unit, he climbed onto the wing and turned the key to open the canopy. He was sitting in the cockpit running an electronics check when Captain Marshall hopped onto the wing to see what was going on.

"We gonna be ready to go in three hours?"

"You just worry about getting her back in one piece. My aircraft will be ready," replied the Chief with an emphasis on the word *my*.

"Okay, Okay. Geez, you sure are getting grumpy in your old age, you really should consider switching to decaff."

The sound of someone clearing his throat caused both men to turn and notice a stern looking major who had mysteriously appeared on the cargo deck. He was trailed by a young lieutenant with a mass of papers and charts.

"I'm Major Hollings, here to give you your final intelligence briefing. Are you sure we can't do this in my office?"

"Uh, sorry sir, no can do," said Marshall hopping down and sketching a quick salute. "I signed for this baby and I'm not about to let her out of my sight until this is all over. I take it I'm about to find out just what 'this' is?"

Marshall guided them over to one of the wide work surfaces attached to the work stations and helped the Lieutenant spread out his charts.

"Higher Authority has asked me to convey their regrets for springing this on you so quickly, but we have quite an opportunity here. As you know, four days ago terrorist bombings occurred at eight U.S. and NATO bases all over the world. What you don't know is that there were supposed to be ten attacks. Two of the terrorist teams were captured, one in the U.S. and one in the U.K. Interrogation and evidence found established an unmistakable link to Libya. Furthermore, both sources confirmed a secret meeting to take place tonight near Benghazi. Apparently, they're planning the next step in their terrorist war on NATO and the heads of terror organizations from all over the world will be in attendance."

"Such as?" Marshall interrupted.

"That's strictly 'Need to Know' information, but I think you can figure it out. We may never get another chance like this. We just broke this yesterday, so there was no time to put together a large raid like we used in '86. After much debate, you and the F-19 were chosen. I don't have to tell you that you'll be totally on your own out there. If you get into trouble, there won't be anyone around to pull your chestnuts out of the fire."

Marshall took a deep breath, "Okay. Let's get on with it."

"Here's the Op." The major handed Marshall several sheets of paper and the lieutenant opened the charts. "Your primary target will be the terrorist camp near Benghazi." He pointed to a spot on the western shore of the Gulf of Sirte, just inside the infamous Line of Death.

"A follow-up strike may be necessary, so your secondary target is the SAM radar site near Al Bayda.

"There are a couple of missile boats in the area, but they're always on the move, so you'll just have to locate them and make adjustments on the way in. There are two permanent SAM locations you'll have to worry about. The first is here," pointing to the chart again, "near Al Bayda airfield. The second is near Benghazi itself."

"What kind?" Asked Marshall without looking up from the notes he was making.

"At Benghazi they've got an SA-5 battery, and at Al Bayda they have SA-2s. Both use older Soviet beam-rider pulse radar technology. They shouldn't be much to worry about. But remember, they scored a hit in '86. Be careful not to drift too far to the south. There's a big SA-12 site in

Maradah with a real nasty doppler system, but it shouldn't be able to pick you up around Benghazi".

"Can't hit what you can't see. What about air cover?"

"They have MiGs operating out of Port Brega, to the south, and Benina, right next to Benghazi. There's one squadron of MiG-23s at Port Brega. The MiG-23 has a lousy search radar. They shouldn't be a problem. But close by at Benina they have MiG-29s. Their search radar is only slightly better than the MiG-23's, but they have excellent maneuverability and better pilots, so be careful around them."

"Weapons?" As Marshall began to get his "game face" on, his questions and comments became terse and to the point.

"The MiG-23s will probably carry AA-7 Apex missiles, both IR and Radar versions. They stink. But the 29s will carry AA-2 Atoll and AA-8 Aphid missiles. Both are pretty good, especially the second generation AA-8s.

"Your fuel estimate is 9,312 pounds. A little tight, but you should be okay if you don't hang around too long."

"What's the ROE?" Marshall knew that the Rules of Engagement would play a big part in how he flew the mission.

"Technically we haven't declared war on Libya, but you're given a full-scale war ROE. You'll have "weapons free" from the time you go "feet wet" over the Med until you land. It seems the brass want to show the F-19 off a little. Of course, they'll deny it officially, but word will get out.

"You have a takeoff window from 2100 to 2105 hours. All the tower knows is that during this time an aircraft will take off or land. They've been advised to not pay too much attention one way or the other."

The major flipped quickly through another couple of pages of notes. "That's about it. You're more or less free to carry out the mission any way you see fit. I'll be whatever help I can. So, what's it gonna be?"

Marshall took a calculator out of his shirt pocket and punched in some numbers. He scratched the stubble on his chin and looked at the map. More numbers in the calculator. He wandered over and got the weapons inventory list from the crew chief. Without looking up, he circled three items and handed it back.

"How's this sound, Major? I think the fuel is a little too tight, so I'll load one bay with an extra fuel cell. That will give me 11,900 pounds. So if I find something interesting, I'll be able to hang around for a while. Two Mavericks will go in another bay for the primary and secondary targets. Those MiG-29s worry me a little, so I'll take four Sidewinders. This still leaves one bay open. Since I've got to fly right past them anyway and there's nothing else worth shooting at, I figured I'd load up with Durandals and take out the two runways."

The major smiled and gave Marshall a wink. "I was hoping you'd say that."

"I always aim to please, Major. Is there some place around here where I can grab a quick shower and a shave? Bad as I smell, I'm afraid I might cause some sort of electronic malfunction in the cockpit!"

"I heard THAT," called Bubba from the cockpit.

"You just get this bird loaded and ready to fight," replied Marshall as he and the major headed down the loading ramp to the tarmac. "Then you can take a little nap while I go do the real work!"

True to his word, the crew chief had the F-19 ready to fly with a half hour to spare. Now with ten minutes left before take-off time, Marshall sat strapped in and ready to go. The Stealth Fighter had been towed from the C-5 after dark and fueled. Then Marshall had taxied to the far end of the airfield, where he now sat with the bay doors open so Bubba could remove the weapon's safety wires just before takeoff.

With nothing to do but sit and wait, Marshall's nerves were beginning to get to him for the first time. He had trained for 15 years to fight but had never actually flown a combat mission. Now all of the doubts he had ever had about being able to "cut it" came rushing back. He knew a pilot's first combat mission was probably the most dangerous. If he could just make it through this one. . . .

He looked at his watch for the tenth time in five minutes and silently said a fighter pilot's prayer: "Please don't let me screw up."

With two minutes to takeoff, Marshall could finally start moving again. He motioned to the crew chief and waited for him to reappear with the safety wires. Bubba ducked out from under the wing and gave him a big OK sign and a sharp salute. As Marshall increased power and taxied to the end of the runway, Bubba hoped he would see both the pilot and aircraft back in one piece.

Marshall turned and brought the plane to a stop at the northern end of the long runway. He applied the brake and extended the flaps. He checked his watch again and at exactly 2100 hours applied full military power. A quick scan of the dials showed all to be in order, so he took a deep breath, reached down with a gloved hand to release the brake, and accelerated down the runway.

The roar of the two GE turbofan engines cracked the cool silence of the Mediterranean night. At 130 knots Marshall pulled back on the stick and brought the nose up. He pulled back a little more, and the dark aircraft was airborne. With full power still on he climbed quickly to 400 feet, snapped the gear up, and leveled off, still on a heading of 180. He cut the throttle back to about 70 percent and turned on the Autopilot. The INS was set to the Primary target, so the plane banked to the right to take the correct course. The white strip of beach flashed past leaving only the black waters of the Mediterranean below him. As the plane leveled out toward Benghazi at 300 knots, Marshall brought the Tactical Situation display up on the left-hand CRT.

Just as he had expected, there were two Libyan missile boats on the prowl. One was broadcasting radar and the other was quiet. "If I'm careful, I should be able to squeeze right between them."

There was activity in the air also; two MiG-23s were patrolling the gap between the boats. A quick check of the EMV scale showed nobody was close to picking him up. But he was getting close to the right-hand missile boat, so he took the stick and turned a little to the west. That put him dead on with the two MiGs. The F-19's first test would come quickly. There was nothing to do but disappear, so he eased forward on the stick and then leveled out at 180 feet. Cutting the

Marshall rotates the F-19 off the runway and nervously heads out for his first taste of combat.

throttle even more, he watched as the EMV indicator got lower and lower. When his speed hit 150 knots, his EMV was so low it was almost off the scale.

A tap of a key changed the HUD to air-to-air mode so he could keep track of the MiGs. Thirty miles out they were painting him with radar but the elusive F-19 was returning a very small signal. It was much too small for the aging MiG radars to pick up. Twenty miles and still no problem. Ten . . . five . . . Marshall held his breath as they flew right over him. He was just about to switch to air-to-ground mode when he noticed one of the MiGs start to turn.

"Aw, come on, no way they could see me!"

But they continued to turn to the east. Marshall eased down to 100 feet. It was bumpy, but keeping the flaps out helped smooth things a little. Just when he was about to increase speed to turn and fight, the two MiGs pulled out of the turn and headed for Al Bayda.

Marshall pulled back up to 400 feet and let out a long breath, "OK, let's get down to business." He switched to air-to-ground mode to take a look around. The airbase at Benina

was the first to show up, then a SAM radar site near Benghazi. He hit the Next Target key and the terrorist camp came up
on the screen with the words PRIMARY TARGET. Another
cool white symbol appeared on the HUD as the Targeting Box
popped up over the camp location. The camp was much big-
ger than he had imagined. It must be air-conditioned, since it's
cool IR signature stood out nicely from the hot desert ground.
The sensitive sensors in the nose of the Maverick missile
should have no problem picking it up. The camp was 45 km
away, and the SAM radar was 50 and a little to the east. He
took a course about half way between the two. At 30 miles
out he cycled through the weapons to bring up the AGM-65D
Maverick missiles. As soon as he did, the targeting box turned
to an oval and TARGET LOCKED flashed on the screen. "Not
yet . . . just a little bit longer."

He expanded the view on the Tactical Display and found
two more MiGs headed his way, probably the same two he
had seen earlier. But the target was only 20 km away; they
would never get there in time. He eased up to 500 feet just as
the targeting oval turned bright red. In one quick motion he
punched the button to open the bay doors, hit the "pickle button" on the stick to launch the missile, and snapped the bay
doors shut again. Marshall looked away to save his night vision as the Maverick leapt off of the rail and streaked away to
the west. He eased forward on the throttle and turned hard to
the east, looking for the SAM radar site. Leveling off at 1200
feet the radar came into view on the CRT. Only 10 km away.

He turned hard to line it up in the center of the HUD. At
6 km he made a minor correction to keep the target centered
and checked the MiGs one more time—they were getting
close. At 3 km away from the radar site he opened the speed-
brake and dived for the target. At the same time a bright flash
was seen to the west, and a message telling him the Maverick
had found its target appeared on the HUD.

Marshall barely noticed it as he concentrated on the spinning radar dish below him. As he passed through 700 feet, he
fired a quick burst from the cannon, which exploded short of
the target, kicking up a fountain of sand. He fired again, now
down to 500 feet; still no good. He fought back the urge to

pull up and fired one more burst. This time he was rewarded with a flash of flames. The blast from the shattered radar lit the desert night. Marshall pulled the stick back into his lap and strained against the mounting G-forces. With only 100 feet to spare, he pulled out of the dive and started a climbing turn to the west, where he knew the frustrated MiG pilots would be investigating the attack on the camp. They would be receiving frantic orders from ground controllers who where even more frustrated. After closing the speed-brake and increasing the throttle to 100 percent, he switched the HUD to air-to-air mode and brought the Sidewinder missiles up. Time to go MiG hunting. "OK, where are ya?"

With the SAM site out of the way, Marshall turns his attention to MiG hunting.

Both MiGs were right where he thought they would be. They were now turning to investigate the latest commotion at the radar site. The first one was only 15 km away and to the right; the second was dead ahead at 20 km. With that much space between them, Marshall figured he could take them out one at a time. He headed toward the first MiG. At 9 km, his EMV indicator beeped to tell him he had been picked up on the MiG's radar, but the tracking light wasn't on so he knew they didn't have a lock on him. It didn't matter anyway; he had a good angle on the MiG from the right and was closing in. The MiG pilot finally saw the F-19 at a range of 5 km and turned hard towards it. But Marshall was ready and put the aircraft over on its side in a hard turn, trying to keep his nose ahead of the target. "Too late, Pal!" Keeping a good lead on the MiG, he fired a short burst from the cannon at 3 km and watched the MiG explode nicely and spiral into the ground.

He pointed the nose toward the ground to try to lose some of the altitude he had gained during the turn, and to pick up some speed. His head bobbed up and down as he alternated between looking out the cockpit and down at the CRT screens. "Where's the other one!" MiG number 2 was closing in from the left and below him. He hit the Cam Left key and the MiG popped up on the screen.

"Gotcha!" Marshall continued the dive and turned toward the enemy. He used the speed he'd gained during the dive to bank over hard and "pull lead" on the second MiG. The range was closing fast and he just had time to squeeze off one quick snap-shot as the MiG flashed past. An explosion and smoke filled the windscreen momentarily as the second pilot joined the first in bailing out.

All this activity had drawn a lot of attention. A check of the Tactical Display showed two more MiGs coming at him at high speed. Marshall's adrenaline was really pumping now. "Come on! Let's see what you got. There's plenty of room to paint two more red stars on the side." He turned toward the attackers and locked the first one up on the CRT—it was a MiG-29. These guys were nothing to fool around with. At 16 km out he opened the bay doors and fired a Sidewinder missile at the first target head-on. Since the target was coming head-on, he knew he'd have to fire early if the missile was to have time to track the target. With the doors still open, he locked up the second MiG, also a 29, and fired another Sidewinder. The two MiG pilots were totally taken by surprise. Both lit their afterburners and turned hard away from the onrushing missiles. "Wrong Move, Boys." The hot afterburners just made a better target for the Sidewinder's IR seeking sensor. Marshall snapped the bay doors shut and pulled out to the west to try and get a little lateral separation just in case the missiles missed. But both missiles found their marks and the planes disappeared from the display with a bright, but silent, flash.

A Sidewinder missile chases after the retreating Mig-29.

With the air clear around him, Marshall took a couple of seconds to get his bearings and plan his next move. Over his shoulder he could see the smoke beginning to rise from where the four burning MiGs had crashed. A feeling of exhilaration washed over him. All his fears were gone. Things had happened so quickly, he had just reacted on instinct and training. And judging by the fresh crop of smoking holes, his instincts were pretty good! Under his oxygen mask, a big grin came over his face as he nosed the plane up and did four quick victory rolls.

Having drawn enough attention to himself, he cut the throttle back and dived for the ground. "Break's over, back to work." The scrap with the MiGs had led him to the west, close to the shore, so he turned back inland and switched to air-to-ground mode. The airbase at Benina came up on the display at 25 km; he adjusted his course to line the targeting box up in the middle of the HUD. Leveling off at 500 feet, he brought the two Durandal runway penetration bombs up. With 12 km to go to the target, he slowed even more and lined the target up. The ends of the red Range Indicator Bar started moving towards the middle of the screen. At 3 km out, Marshall opened the bay doors. He made a nice, slow, level pass over the runway at 500 feet and released the bomb as the ends of the range bar met.

The Durandal dropped from the weapons bay and deployed a small parachute. It hung nose-down over the runway for a moment; then the rocket motor in the tail burst to life, shooting the warhead deep into the concrete surface. Once well under the tarmac, the warhead exploded, sending huge slabs of concrete into the air. It would be quite some time before anyone took off or landed at Benina. Any MiG-29s that hadn't been damaged in the blast would be grounded until the runway was patched.

A good Durandal hit should keep this runway out of action for awhile.

A loud tone from the EMV indicator brought Marshall's head back down into the cockpit. The SAM radar site just past the runway, which had been quiet, had just been fired up and had spotted him. Pushing the throttle to the stops, he turned hard toward the site, which was only 5 km away. Pulling the nose up, he managed to clear 800 feet by the time he was 3 km from the radar. Extending the speed-brake he dived for the target, hoping to blind the site by destroying its radar before it could fire on him. Marshall lined the radar up in a shallow dive and started firing. His first shells were way short but found one of the missile launchers, which exploded beneath him. He continued to fire long bursts and walked his fire onto the radar, which also exploded nicely. "Must be my lucky day." Since this dive had been shallow, the pull out wasn't so bad. He checked the throttle, pulled in the brake, and headed north, leaving a stunned Libyan air force in his wake.

He slowed down to 200 knots and skimmed along 180 feet above the desert floor. A bright flash on the EMV scale showed the SAM radar at Al Bayda was up and operating. As he moved northward, the signals became stronger. But hugging the ground paid off. At 32 km the Maverick acquired the Secondary Target and the TARGET LOCKED message came up again on the CRT. He watched the radar dish casually spinning on the Track Cam CRT and closed in for the kill. At 20 klicks, he popped up to 500 feet. He was just shy of being seen now. But before the radar could paint him again, he opened the bay doors and sent the Maverick on its way. Ten seconds later the dish disappeared in a flash of smoke and flames. A quick turn to the right and the airstrip at Al Bayda came up on the screen.

"One last chore." A wide scan of the Tactical Display showed another MiG in the area, apparently headed for Al Bayda. Both the range to the MiG and the range to the targeted runway were closing quickly. It was going to be close.

Marshall climbed to 600 feet as the screen showed ten km to the target. He brought the other Durandal up and adjusted his course to line up with the targeting diamond. He was going so slowly that even at 600 feet the MiG couldn't pick him up on radar. Not yet. The Range Indicator Bars were marching steadily towards the center of the HUD when the EMV gauge beeped. The MiG had spotted him. But he was too close to the target to pull off now. The MiG-23 was pulling around on his tail as he opened the doors and released the Durandal for another direct hit.

But there was no time for celebration. The MiG slid in behind the F-19 and fired an AA-2 Atoll missile. Marshall hit max power as the missile launch message came up on the HUD. At the same time the Red IR indicator started to flash. An AA-2 wasn't the greatest missile in the world, but when fired straight up your tailpipe it was hard to shake. Marshall gritted his teeth as he fought the temptation to turn hard, waiting for his airspeed to build. Finally at 300 knots he could wait no longer. A loud klaxon sounded, the missile was only seconds away. "Now!" After popping a flare he rolled the dark aircraft over and turned as hard as he could, yanking the stick back into his lap. Ignoring the G-forces and the Stall Warning, he held the turn until the Atoll shot harmlessly past him.

The tight turn had bled away most of his airspeed, and he struggled against a stall as he pulled out of the turn. But the stall was a disguised blessing as the MiG pilot scrambled in the cockpit and was forced to overshoot.

"OK, pal, it's your turn now!"

Once again the bay doors whined open. Heart pounding, he turned towards the MiG that was racing away and sent a Sidewinder missile after it. The race was on. The MiG pilot went to afterburner in an attempt to outrun the missile. Marshall watched on the Tactical Display as the Sidewinder slowly made up ground. "Go Baby, Go!" Just when it looked as if the Sidewinder would run out of steam, the two images on the screen met. Marshall had the MiG on the Track Cam and noticed the MiG pilot was taking no chances. Just before the missile hit, he bailed out.

"Well, it's been a blast gang, but I'm afraid I'm gonna have to break up this little party and make tracks for home." Marshall transferred the fuel from the extra tank in the weapons bay to the main tank with a couple of quick keystrokes.

He had plenty to spare. Cutting the throttles back to 70 percent, he turned and headed due north, back out over the water.

As the narrow strip of beach passed under him at 400 feet, Marshall gave the transmit button on the stick four clicks. This was the signal to those listening nervously to all the angry chatter on Libyan radio that he was once again "feet wet" and headed for home.

A bright flash on the EMV scale announced the presence of the two Libyan missile boats. Instinctively, Marshall nosed down and cut his throttle. He leveled off at 150 feet and surveyed the situation and his options. With no missiles left and only a couple of hundred rounds of cannon ammo, he decided to leave those two fish for someone else. "I guess I bagged the limit tonight." He waited for the next radar pulse, and then banked hard to the east as soon as it passed. Before the next pulse could reach him, he pulled out of the turn and leveled the wings on his new course. With plenty of fuel on board, it just made sense not to push his luck and simply fly around the threat.

Marshall made a pistol with his finger and pointed it off to the west toward the closest boat. "Not tonight fellas, not tonight."

The Stealth Pilot Papers
OPERATION: Federal Express

OPERATION: Federal Express

Captain Marshall paced nervously in the makeshift ready room, pausing occasionally to stare out the window into the moonless night. He had spent three days and nights confined to the hanger facility at the Ras Shaffaniyah airstrip along the northern coast of Saudi Arabia. It wasn't that the accommodations weren't nice—quite the contrary. Some of the richest men in the world came and went through these facilities as they conducted their business dealings at the oil terminal. Luxury was a way of life for the "haves" in this part of the world. It was the waiting that was getting to the captain. Three times he had been briefed and ready to go, and three times someone in Washington had pulled the plug at the last minute.

Part of the frustration came from the fact that he thought it was such a simple mission. Sneak in, land, pick up a package, and leave a little calling card on the way out. Piece of cake. All Marshall knew about the package was that it had something to do with Soviet high-energy particle beam research. It had been smuggled out of Russia and, in what the intelligence community thought was a brilliant plan, smuggled into Iran. The Soviets were frantically searching along their border with Afghanistan, a natural escape route. The CIA figured Iran would seem to be the last place they would try to set up operations. And though it was hardly ideal, they did have access to a secret rebel airstrip deep in the Zagros Mountains.

All Marshall had to do was show up during a particular time window and pick it up. But the package was late arriving—they preferred to refer to it as late rather than missing. They were all visibly worried. Marshall's main worry was that the longer he stayed there with his highly unusual fighter, the better the chances were the mission would be compromised.

He picked up the small clipboard that would ride on his thigh during the flight and carried it over to the large confer-

133

ence table covered with maps and charts. He double checked his notes, wondering again if there was anything he had missed. The flight plan was simple, but if anyone found out he was here it would also be obvious. The thought of flying into a trap did not sit well on a stomach that had been subjected to three days of Arabic cuisine. He was to fly through a small gap in radar coverage between Bandar Khomenyi and Bushehr. Both had good U.S.-made Hawk Doppler surface-to-air missile radar systems. Once through the gap he would be in a desolate section of the Zagros Mountains that wasn't covered by radar but was surrounded by enemy airbases. Once north of Bandar Khomenyi and Bushehr with their squadrons of F-5s, he would have Esfahan airbase to the north with two squadrons of F-4Es and Shiraz to the east with Iran's lone squadron of lethal U.S.-made F-14 Tomcats. He didn't relish the thought of tangling with them.

The intelligence spooks were still calling this a combat mission, although during the wait several spineless members of congress who were informed of the mission had gotten cold feet about the strike portion. Iran had recently put into service on Kharg Island a new generation of Silkworm missiles purchased from China. This new version had a larger rocket assist during the launch phase of the missile's flight, which greatly increased the effective range. With a rumored range of almost 200 miles, this put all shipping in the northern gulf in jeopardy. But even more frightening to the pro-U.S. nations of Kuwait, Bahrain, and Qatar was the thought of these missiles raining death and destruction upon their cities. The original plan had been for Marshall to hit this site on his way out of Iran. But the longer they waited, the greater the chance that someone on Capitol Hill would get popsicle toes.

The lanky IO (Intelligence Officer) stuck his head in the door. "Time to suit up; looks like we may go this time." That's what he said the last three times, thought Marshall, as he started his preflight ritual. The CIA only had radio contact with the secret airstrip once a day. Marshall had to be in the F-19 and ready to go when the contact was made. If the package was there, he would launch immediately. There was a good chance someone was tracking the party with the package. The longer they had to sit at the airstrip, the better the chances were they might have uninvited guests.

Marshall started to sort through the pile of survival gear in the corner of the room. He pulled his G-suit over his "plain Jane" flight suit, which had no insignia or name tag. He struggled into his yellow life vest and headed for the john. Few things in life are as uncomfortable as the combination of a full bladder and high Gs.

Ready to go, he attached the small clipboard to his thigh, grabbed his gloves and helmet bag, and headed out into the hanger. His crew chief, Master Sergeant Bubba Spencer, had just finished his preflight prep of the sleek black F-19 and was putting on another pot of coffee.

"Gonna go flyin' today, Boss?" asked Bubba, as he handed the captain the aircraft acceptance form to sign.

"Your guess is as good as mine, Bubba." Marshall signed the paperwork and began his walk-around of the aircraft to check the control surfaces and look for leaks.

"Well, I hear it's a go this time, sir."

"Sounds good to me." Although still skeptical, Marshall had learned to trust Bubba's information. Wherever they went in the world, Bubba would tap into the most up-to-date informational database in the military, the sergeant's grapevine. Sergeants seemed to always know what was going on before the officers did.

Marshall finished his walk-around and scrambled up the ladder to the cockpit. Bubba followed him up to help get him strapped in. "I tell you Boss, you're gonna go."

Marshall yelled down to the CIA man who always seemed to show up when Bubba made a fresh pot of coffee. "What's the latest on the strike option?"

"It seems that the DCI is having a hard time catching up to the congressmen in question. So until I hear otherwise, it's on." In actuality, the DCI (Director of Central Intelligence) was playing an intense game of hide and seek in Washington, hoping the mission would start before those particular congress members could find *him*.

With the auxiliary power unit fired up, Marshall punched a button and the cockpit avionics blinked to life. He activated the BITE (Built-In Test Equipment) and watched as they ran through their computer checks. Once completed, he brought up the Internal Navigation System. After waiting a minute for the INS gyros to spin up, he punched in the coordinates of Ras Shaffaniya to let the plane know where it was. When the correct map popped up on the left-hand display, he moved the cursor to set the waypoints to his chosen flight path. Everything checked out ready to go. There was nothing to do now but wait.

When the CIA man was satisfied the F-19 was ready to go, he headed for the radio room to try and make contact with the rebel airstrip. A few minutes later he reappeared in the doorway, made a circle in the air with his thumb and finger, and disappeared again. Bubba hit a button to kill the red night working lights and opened both the large hanger doors as Marshall started to spool up the two big turbojet engines. He took his helmet out of the blue bag with "The Judge" blazed across the side in red, put it on, and plugged it in. The roar of the GE turbojets made conversation impossible, so Bubba put on a headset and plugged it into the undercarriage of the jet. "See Boss, I told you!" he shouted over the roar of the engines.

"I'm not airborne yet, Bubba."

The intelligence officer appeared at the door and waved Bubba over. After a few quick words, he gave the captain a quick salute and disappeared.

"Like I said Boss, it's a go. Good luck and Godspeed, sir." He stepped back, unhooked his headset, came to ramrod attention, and gave the captain a sharp salute.

Marshall's gloved hand returned the salute crisply and then eased the throttle forward. The F-19 rolled out of the hanger. Once clear of the doors, he stopped the rolling aircraft to check the brakes and to arm the ejection seat. The seat was always left unarmed when the aircraft was in a hanger—you wouldn't want it to accidentally shoot you through the roof. He moved the stick and watched over his shoulder as all the control surfaces moved correctly. He raised and lowered the dorsal fin-like speed brake. Three blinks from a light in the tower told him he was free to taxi.

After running through the checklist, Marshall taxis toward the runway.

He advanced the throttle a little more and drove quickly to the end of the runway, feeling naked and exposed on the ground. A rapid 180-degree turn and he was ready to go. Without even a pause, he extended his flaps and pushed the throttle to the stops. Blue flame shot out of the rear of the strange-looking aircraft as it lurched forward and rumbled down the runway. At 130 knots he pulled back on the stick, and the ride got suddenly smooth as the gear left the tarmac. Finally, Operation Federal Express was underway.

Once airborne, he immediately cleaned up the aircraft by snapping up the landing gear. A quick punch on the keyboard engaged the autopilot while he cycled through his weapons and brought up the Tactical Display screen. This screen would be constantly updated by a circling E-3C Airborne Early Warning and Control aircraft. The E-3C couldn't come to his aid, but it could provide him with a much better picture of what was going on in the area than his enemy would have.

This was going to be a walk in the park, thought Marshall, as he scanned the instruments and started to settle into his flying routine. As the craft leveled out at 495 feet, the updated display came up. This was his first indication that everything might not go as planned. The gap in radar coverage he had planned to exploit had been filled by three patrolling missile boats.

"Well, they never said this was going to be easy." Still, on the other side of the Persian Gulf and over a hundred kilometers away, it was hard to tell just how close together the patrol boats were. But since they carried the older pulse-type radar, Marshall figured he could get around them somehow.

Just as Marshall was beginning to get comfortable again, the situation went from bad to worse as the E-3C reported aircraft taking off from both Bandar Khomenyi and Bushehr, probably F-5s. They quickly appeared on the Tactical Display headed out over the gulf. Moments later they were joined by a third aircraft, possibly an F-14 from Shiraz. It was Marshall's worst nightmare. Either the Iranians were incredibly lucky or the long delay had given someone the opportunity to locate him. Either way, things were going to be very difficult from here on in.

Marshall also figured if they knew about him, then the team at the secret airfield was in even more danger. The sooner he could get there and pick up the package, the sooner they could disappear into the safety of the rugged Zagros Mountains.

He disengaged the autopilot and reduced the throttle to about 60 percent. Pushing forward on the stick, he eased the aircraft down to 200 feet, then to 150. The pitch black waters of the gulf slid silently past beneath him. Switching to air-to-air mode he picked up the first F-5 on the TrackCam. It was moving at 600 knots. The three aircraft appeared to be moving to take up patrol positions in front of the missile boats—a nice, layered defense. He cycled through the other aircraft, confirming they were indeed another F-5 and an F-14.

Marshall pushed his loose oxygen mask aside and scratched his chin while he weighed his options. He could attack the aircraft and one of the missile boats to clear his path, but doing so would alert everyone to his presence and get a lot more aircraft in the air looking for him. Other radar operators would also be much more alert or they might wake up the first team operators. He would much rather slip in without being seen and stir things up on the way out. He decided to try the quiet approach first.

The F-14 worried Marshall more than the others. It had an excellent doppler air-to-air radar and only the best pilots got to fly them. The F-5s were equipped with older pulse-type radars, easy to sneak by but tough in a tight battle. The F-14 had taken up a position in between the F-5s. "That's where I would have put it," thought Marshall. It was patrolling in a clockwise direction, so Marshall eased the stick to the left. He planned to try and sneak behind the F-14 to the left and then do his best to avoid the F-5 to that side.

The F-14 pulled out of a turn and was pointing directly at the F-19. Marshall eased the stick forward and took the plane down to 100 feet in preparation for the coming radar sweep. He watched the EMV scale as the pulse from the F-14 made a bright blue bar that extended about halfway down the scale. It was strong but still had a ways to go before it would detect him. His EMV was hugging the bottom of the scale.

Immediately after the pulse, he turned a little to the right to try and get out of the cone of radar coverage in front of the aircraft as quickly as possible. The next pulse came. It was

Stay cool and sneak under this fighter patrol.

stronger than the first but still not strong enough to pick up the slow-moving F-19. The range was only 30 km when the F-14 passed in front of Marshall moving right to left in its race-track search pattern. He tried to slide in behind it, hoping he could make it past him before he came around the pattern again. He increased the throttle to try and keep up with the faster fighter.

The F-5 on that side was getting uncomfortably close. A pulse from his radar was almost to the detection level, so Marshall gritted his teeth and backed off the throttle to reduce his radar signature. His heart pounded the seconds away as he waited for the F-5 to turn. But it kept on coming straight towards him.

BONK! A yellow flash on the EMV scale and the warning tone told him the F-5 had picked up his radar return. It probably had not located him yet, but it was close. Marshall increased the throttle a little and turned hard heading straight for the F-5. He was trying to get past him and out of his radar cone before the next pulse. Besides, pulse radars were best fooled by flying straight at them. At least that was the theory.

He pulled out of the turn and leveled his wings just before the next pulse. This time it showed up as a blue bar on the scale. It was close to seeing him but still in the safe range. The F-5 flashed by him on his right before the next pulse. Marshall took a deep breath and rubbed his eyes. He was out of danger for the moment.

BONK! His break was short lived as another warning tone sounded. Shocked, he looked quickly to the EMV scale. This time he had been spotted by a ground-based radar. A check of his altitude showed why. During his hard turns to avoid the F-5, he had wandered up to 500 feet and into the radar coverage zone of the Hawk Doppler system at Bandar Khomenyi. "Rookie mistake," he grumbled, as he cut the throttle and dove for the deck. When the next pulse came, it went all the way down the scale but stopped just short of the detection threshold. Reducing his speed and altitude had done the trick. Marshall immediately increased the throttle and turned hard away from the radar source, just managing to pull out before the next pulse. Two more seconds and it would have had him.

He took a course headed due east; this took him away from the threatening Hawk SAM battery but right back into the teeth of the three patrolling aircraft, all of which seemed to be heading straight towards him.

"Well, when your plan doesn't work, you make a new plan." Marshall cycled through his weapons to arm the three AMRAMM radar-guided missiles in bay number 3 and snapped his oxygen mask firmly into place.

Three against one weren't his favorite odds but he would be able to get off the first shot. Words from flight training came back to him. "Lose sight, lose fight." He could see them and they couldn't see him, not yet at least. Marshall's fingers played the keyboard and locked onto the first target, an F-5 Tiger II. He wanted to take this first bogey by surprise. Opening his bay doors to use a missile would probably give his position away so he elected to go after the first bogey with his cannon.

He pushed the throttle to the wall and started a shallow left turn to keep the Tiger in his 12 o'clock position. With over a thousand knots closure speed, the target grew rapidly in the aiming circle on the HUD. Marshall was going to shoot him in the face with a frontal cannon shot. The Tiger veered slightly to the left, still unaware of the danger, but Marshall stayed padlocked on the F-5's course.

When the range fell to 8 km, Marshall put the "death dot" gun aiming circle a little ahead of the target and squeezed the first burst of cannon fire. He banked to the left to pull a little more lead on the bogey and squeezed off another burst of 50 cannon shells. He felt, more than heard, the burr of the gatling cannon as it filled the sky in front of the Tiger with a curtain of exploding steel. His timing had been good and the Tiger flew right through the deadly sheet of fire. It's left wing tip and stabilizer went immediately; then it burst into flames and cartwheeled into cold black water.

"One down!" Marshall burst through the smoke trail left by the burning F-5 and reefed the stick back into a hard climbing right turn. The other two bogeys were just now aware of his presence and adjusted their headings. Still turning hard to the right at 5000 feet, Marshall rolled inverted and

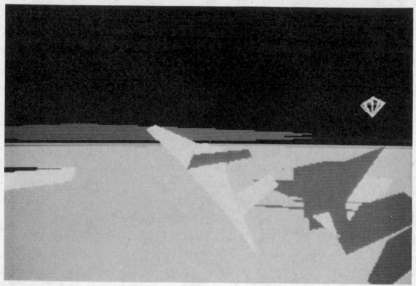

There's no kill like a guns kill!

pointed the nose below the horizon to gain speed. The other two bogeys now came into view below him and to his right. He pulled back hard on the stick and fought the climbing G-forces as his turn tightened.

The F-14 popped up on the TrackCam at the same instant the warning tone sounded: It had radar lock on him. The yellow TRACK light flashed its warning as the bay doors whined opened beneath the F-19. A short pylon extended below the aircraft and the AMRAAM missiles attached came alive to search for a target. Marshall held his tight turn until the words TARGET LOCKED appeared on the TrackCam CRT. With that he squeezed the trigger and an AMRAAM leapt off the rail after the Tomcat. At almost the same instant a bright plume appeared under the wing of the F-14 as an AIM-7 Sparrow missile set out in search of Marshall's Stealth Fighter.

The hard turn had bled away a great deal of Marshall's airspeed, so he had no choice but to dive for the deck if he wanted to have enough speed to avoid the incoming missile. A flashing yellow *R* on the right-hand console told him the missile's robot brain had located him and was tracking. He started a shallow turn to the right during the dive to try and force the missile off to his side. Sweat rolled down his face and off the tip of his oxygen mask as he watched the altimeter unwind in a blur. At 200 feet he pulled up. The missile was now directly off to his right. In one quick motion, he leveled the wings, punched out two blooms of chaff, and dipped down to 100 feet. Behind him, millions of small strips of metal swirled into a cloud in his slipstream. It made a much nicer target than the radar elusive fighter, so the missile released the F-19 and exploded harmlessly in the chaff.

The AMRAAM was still tracking the F-14 when Marshall got around to checking the Tactical Display. He cheered the missile on as it made up ground on the gyrating fighter. Just as the two images met on the display, Marshall saw a welcome flash off to the right. But a bright blue flash on the EMV scale showed the Tomcat had decoyed the missile and was still alive and hunting, but it had lost the F-19 in the confusion. The other F-5 never located the elusive Stealth Fighter and was circling over the burning oil slick that marked the final resting place of his partner.

A quick check of his watch told Marshall that he was dangerously behind schedule. Though he had taken out only one of the bogeys, the resulting melee had put him to the north of the fighters and back on route. The circling F-5 would certainly make an easy target, but he forced himself to think of the team desperately waiting for him at the airstrip. "Mission first."

He turned his attention to the three missile boats that now blocked his path. He zoomed in the Map view on the left-hand CRT to take a look at the boat's radar activity. A pulse from the boat to the west flashed about halfway down the EMV scale. It was followed by a similar pulse from the boat to the east. But the boat dead ahead remained quiet. Marshall watched and waited. Still nothing.

"Maybe I'll finally get a break," thought Marshall as he considered the situation. He should be able to slip between the radar coverage with no problem, but not without passing very close to the silent boat in the middle. If its radar was broken, he could blast right by with no problem. But if it was

143

only shut down and they heard him pass overhead, they could launch a SAM at him from dangerously close range.

"Nope, I've taken enough chances for one night. Let's make this one a sure thing." Marshall checked his gun ammo and decided to make sure the boat stayed quiet.

The stocky Stealth Fighter pilot adjusted his course to head straight for the missile boat and eased forward on the throttle. He approached, clipping the wave tops at 300 knots. At a range of 6 km, he started a climb up to 1000 feet. Marshall was surprised to see that the boat still had its running lights on as he extended the speed brake, nosed over, and started to dive on the unsuspecting warship. Bright lights against the dark water made a perfect target. The jet and wind noise faded away as Marshall concentrated on keeping the boat under the aiming circle on the HUD. He was faintly aware of the altitude numbers on the right side of the HUD. When 600 feet flashed by, he squeezed the trigger and felt the aircraft shudder as the 20mm cannon spit out 50 rounds in less than a second. An eruption of white foam in front of the boat signaled a miss so Marshall squeezed the trigger again. This group of shells ripped into the boat and taught the ship's captain a hard lesson about storing munitions on the deck.

Scratch one missile boat.

The exploding cannon shells would have caused enough damage to put the boat out of commission for a week or so, but one of the shells touched off a much larger warhead on the deck and the entire stern disappeared in a cloud of splinters.

Yanking the stick back as far as it would go, Marshall grunted against the mounting Gs and leveled off at 1000 feet. He pulled in the speed brake and fire-walled the throttle. The bright explosion would certainly draw a lot of fighter attention—best be gone when they arrived.

With the burning hulk of the missile boat 30 km behind him, Marshall approached the Iranian coast. The two strong Hawk radar sites were to his right and left and getting closer, so he cut the throttle to 60 percent and tried to hold a constant 150 feet of altitude. He had to be very careful and hit the gap just right. The radar at Bushehr swept his way and left a blue bar about three-quarters of the way down the scale. It was followed shortly by a pulse from the Bandar Khomenyi site; it seemed a little stronger. Hoping to stay in the middle, Marshall veered a little to the east towards Bushehr. The next pair of pulses were about equal in strength but much closer to the detection threshold. The pair that followed were closer still. Marshall began to have evil thoughts about the intelligence officer who claimed there was a gap in the radar coverage. "No problem" he had said. "You could drive a C-5 through there." We're going to have a real interesting debriefing if I live through this, he thought.

The next pulse from Bushehr was almost all the way down the scale. Marshall blinked the sweat from his eyes and reduced the throttle further. The airspeed rolled down past 150 knots, and he eased down to 100 feet. The speed dropped to 140 and kept falling. The next pulse flashed down the scale but stayed blue. They didn't see him.

A strip of white breakers signaled the water's edge. Marshall was glad to finally be over land. Perhaps the ground clutter would degrade the radar performance. He was starting to feel a little more confident when a small blinking light up ahead caught his attention. At first he thought it was a helicopter slightly above him, but it didn't seem to be moving. . . .

"Oil derrick!" Reacting purely on instinct, he turned so

hard to the right that his head almost bounced off the canopy. Flying knife-edged, he just skimmed by the 150-foot structure with the stall warning klaxon screaming in his face. Acutely aware of the ground rushing by beneath him, his left hand jammed the throttle to the stops as he jerked the wings level with his right. Marshall winced and held his breath as the altimeter spun down to double digits. Thrust and lift fought with gravity in a deadly race. With barely 50 feet between the hardscrabble surface of the desert and the sleek black undercarriage of the F-19, lift won out and the altimeter reversed direction.

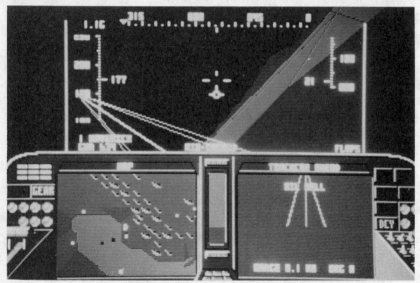

That blinking light turns out to be an oil derrick!

Leveling off at 200 feet, he took a second to catch his breath and check the situation. The next radar pulse from Bushehr was a little weaker than before. He checked his position on the map and found he was past the two radar sites and moving into safer territory. Several aircraft were in the air behind him, but none seemed to be headed his way. A check of the luminous green dial on his watch told him he needed to make up some time if he was going to make it to the secret airstrip on time. With the radar pulses getting fainter, he increased the throttle. WAYPOINT 1 REACHED flashed on the HUD and the NAV cursor jumped 20 degrees to the left. Marshall put the plane into a gentle bank and pulled out on the new heading.

After 20 minutes at 400 knots, Marshall could make out the dark crags of the Zagros Mountains against the horizon. He had made up the proper amount of time, so he backed off on the throttle, not knowing exactly how much further he would have to go before landing. The mountains loomed larger ahead of him, but there was still nothing on the TrackCam.

Finally, the right-hand CRT blinked and the lighted runway appeared on the screen. Range, 30 km. Marshall maintained his course of 335 degrees and watched as the target box on the HUD and the NAV cursor moved slowly to his right. When the NAV cursor slid under the 000 marker on the HUD, he turned back hard and lined it up in the center of the screen. With a few minor corrections, he had the NAV cursor in the center of the screen and was on a heading of 000. Since he knew the runway was lined up due north, he should be in line for landing.

"Yikes!" said the Captain unconsciously as the landing strip came into visual range. The strip was nestled right up against the base of a mountain, and it was short, too. He would only get one try at landing. There was just not enough room off the end of the runway to pull up and go around without smashing into the face of the cliff. One way in and one way out. He eased up to 500 feet to get a better picture of his lineup, dropped his gear, and eased the throttle back to 50 percent. At ten km out, he started his descent. Marshall was aiming for the very end of the runway, as he knew he would need every foot in order to stop.

200 feet . . . four km out. 100 at 2 km. The runway was coming up quickly. He was down to 20 feet when the end of the strip rushed under him. As soon as his wheels touched the ground he cut the throttle back, applied the brakes, and prayed it would stop in time. It rolled to a stop with 50 feet to spare, staring at the rocky face of the mountain only another 200 feet beyond.

Inching the throttle forward slightly, Marshall taxied the

F-19 to the end of the runway and turned it around, ready to take off again. Over to his left he could make out something moving beyond the runway lights and a moment later a jeep pulled through the lights and onto the tarmac. "I sure hope these are the good guys," Marshall thought, as he sat with his hand on the throttle, ready to take off at the first sign of trouble. He blinked his landing lights twice. The driver of the jeep blinked his twice in return, then twice more. That was the okay signal, so Marshall flipped a switch and the canopy whined open, letting in the cool night air.

The jeep pulled alongside the oddly shaped fighter and four heavily armed black-clad men jumped out. Marshall watched over the lip of the canopy as one of them approached the F-19. With the engines still running at idle, it was much too noisy to converse, but a big smile and a sharp salute were all the communications necessary. Marshall reached over with his right hand, pushed a series of buttons, and the doors to bay number 1 slid open.

The other three men grabbed an oblong crate from the rear of the jeep and disappeared under the fighter. After a few moments, they reappeared and the leader gave Marshall a thumbs up. With that, Marshall closed the bay doors and extended a gloved hand down from the cockpit. The black clad figure below smiled and reached up. With Marshall straining against his straps and the man on the ground standing on tiptoe, they managed a quick handshake. Marshall mouthed the words "Thank you" over the din of the jet engines. The other man backed away shaking his head and smiling. "Thank *you*," he shouted, pointing up to the pilot. Then he and the others disappeared into the night.

Not wanting to wear out his welcome, Marshall checked to make sure the brake was on and ran the throttle up to full military power. When the power level reached 100 percent, he released the brake and felt the surge of acceleration as he rocketed down the barren strip. He kept the nose down as long as possible, building up speed. Finally, just as he was about to run out of runway, he pulled the stick back and the aircraft leapt into the air. The howl of the engines ripped through the quiet mountain night and echoed through the cracks and canyons. By the time the quiet returned and the local hillsmen came to investigate, the four men on the ground would be miles away.

Marshall snapped the gear up and flipped on the autopilot while he selected the next waypoint and ran a check on the two Maverick air-to-ground missiles in bay number 2. "Enough with the hide and seek. It's time to come out of hiding." He banked the aircraft to follow the new course indicated by the NAV cursor. It would take him straight to Bushehr. The secondary target was the Silkworm missile site on Kharg Island, but it was so close to Bushehr that it was just easier to take out the SAM radar at Bushehr on the way to Kharg Island.

Marshall weaves his way out of the rugged Zagros Mountains.

Weaving his way out of the mountains, Marshall settled onto a low and slow path to Bushehr. He was picking up radar pulses from the Hawk site again, but they were only half way down the scale. An F-5 circled to the west, but Marshall easily snuck past its weak radar system.

The lights of the busy city glowed on the horizon. There was port activity round the clock, and there would be a great deal more activity shortly. Cycling through the targets avail-

able on the TrackCam, Marshall viewed the downtown area
and the airfield, and finally locked onto the Hawk SAM
site. Range 40 km. He eased down to 150 feet as the radar
pulses became stronger. At 36 km the targeting box on the
HUD changed to an oval and the words TARGET LOCKED
flashed on the TrackCam view. But he couldn't risk a long
range shot; he only had two Mavericks, and he had to make
both count.

The next radar sweep came at 28 km and greeted the pilot
with a loud BONK from the radar warning indicator. Seeing
no use in being coy any longer, Marshall jammed the throttles
forward. BONK! The radar site had him now as the Trak light
started to flash. Up ahead the captain saw a bright flash as a
Hawk missile leapt off its launcher and raced after him at one
and a half times the speed of sound. The captain's mouth got
suddenly dry as he envisioned a missile the size of a telephone pole rocketing after him. He wanted to take evasive action, but he had to maintain this course long enough to launch
the Maverick or he would be dodging SAMs all night.

A quick keystroke zoomed in the view on the Tactical
Display so he could see when the missile got close. At 20 km
to the target he opened the bay doors and nervously fingered
the fire button as the SAM continued to fly straight towards
him. 18 km and he could see the SAM glowing dead ahead.
Determined to wait, he gritted his teeth and watched. Finally
at 16 km, with the SAM bearing down on him, he pressed the
button on the control stick and the Maverick left the bay,
streaming out after the radar site. With the missile warning
klaxon blaring in his helmet, Marshall released a radar decoy
and yanked the F-19 hard to the left.

His timing was almost perfect. The SAM immediately
went after the decoy and exploded with a bright yellow flash
behind the aircraft. Marshall felt the aircraft buck as the shock
wave hit him. But the Hawk is a big missile and has a large
kill zone. Though just out of the kill area, the F-19 still collect-
ed several of the small iron rods flung out by the missile's det-
onation. Marshall growled angrily as several of the green
lights on the Damage Board went to red. The first thing he noticed was a reduction in power. One of the engines must have

taken a hit. He seemed to be using fuel a little faster, too. "This isn't good. Nope, Bubba's not going to like this one little bit." His spirits were lifted by the flash of an explosion up ahead and a message saying the SAM site had been destroyed.

But his spirits plummeted again when that message was replaced with, HAWK MISSILE LAUNCHED FROM KHARG ISLAND. The missile quickly appeared on the Tactical Display. Marshall turned the F-19 so he was flying perpendicular to its path. While waiting for the missile to close on him, he scanned the area with the TrackCam and locked onto the Silkworm missile site only 30 km away on Kharg Island.

He continued to turn, keeping the missile in his three o'clock position until his warning klaxon sounded. This time he would do it by the book. He punched out a bale of chaff and switched on the ECM (Electronic CounterMeasures) to jam the radar. The yellow *R* stopped flashing, indicating the missile had lost its lock. Marshall grunted and pulled a six-G turn toward the missile, forcing it to overshoot. He immediately shut down the ECM and dove for the ground to pick up speed. The turn put his nose back on the Silkworm battery, with the range now only 20 km. A quick check of the Tactical

The last missile eliminates a troublesome Silkworm Missile site.

Display showed more trouble in the form of two aircraft heading his way. Add to that another SAM launch, and things were not looking good for the stocky Air Force captain.

The targeting oval turned to red and Marshall let go his last Maverick against the Silkworm missile installation. That out of the way, he turned his attention back to the incoming aircraft and missile. With the missile in front and the aircraft to his right, Marshall turned to head straight for the aircraft. A burst of flame on the island and a message showed him that the Maverick had found its mark. A pillar of smoke lifted into the air as the fire roared at the missile site. Small secondary explosions followed as missile warheads began to cook off in the fire.

With the SAM now closing in on his tail and the two bogeys dead ahead, Marshall popped off his second decoy drone and headed for low altitude. The SAM as well as both aircraft locked onto the decoy right away as the F-19 slipped off to the right. The decoy still had ten seconds of life when both aircraft, an F-5 and an F-14, passed by him on the left. This was enough time for Marshall to whip around and get on their tails. He wasted no time in opening the bay doors and launching a hungry Sidewinder missile after each plane. Fired from less than 5 km, both Iranian pilots had little time to react. They scrambled in their cockpits to take evasive action, but at mach three the Sidewinders ate up the range in a hurry. Before the enemy pilots could maneuver to safety, the growling Sidewinders homed in on the hot jet exhaust and exploded, ripping large sheets of metal off the planes and sending them spiraling into the sea.

Fighting the temptation to run for home at full speed, Marshall took a deep breath, nosed down to 150 feet, and eased off the throttle until his airspeed dropped to 150 knots. At that altitude and speed, the shocked radar operators watched in disbelief as he suddenly disappeared from the screens. More planes would be vectored to his last known location, but he would be long gone by the time they arrived.

The next waypoint was set for the home base, but a couple of quick calculations and a check of the fuel bar showed that at the current rate of consumption, he would never make it. The quick fight had taken him back up to the northwest. A check of the map showed he had only one option.

Reluctantly, Marshall thumbed the mike switch on the control stick and broke radio silence for the first time. "Watchtower, Banshee 1." The circling E-3A was using the call sign Watchtower; Marshall was Banshee 1.

A somewhat surprised female controller came back over the radio, "Roger, Banshee 1. Read you five by five. Go ahead."

"Declaring minor damage and minimum fuel. Request priority handling into Second Base." Second base was the code name for the alternate return route landing site, which in this case was Kuwait City Airport. While not exactly a U.S. ally, Kuwait was certainly in favor of the U.S. presence in the gulf. A request for an emergency landing could hardly be denied, especially at this late hour when the airport wasn't busy.

"Banshee 1, Watchtower. Fly heading two-seven-zero. Wait one for landing clearance."

"Roger, Watchtower." Marshall banked lazily over to 270 degrees and activated the TrackCam view to the right to lock in Kuwait City Airport.

"Banshee 1, Watchtower. Are you requesting emergency equipment at this time?"

Marshall thought for a moment. He hated to cause such a commotion. But with leaking fuel and hydraulic fluid, it was better to be safe than sorry. "That's affirmative, Watchtower."

"Banshee 1, you're cleared to land. Jump to Air Traffic Control frequency."

"Roger, Watchtower. Hats off to ya. Thanks for the help." Marshall reached over to the radio frequency knob, but before he turned it he keyed the mike once more. "Watchtower, Banshee 1. Next time you stop at Home Plate, I'm buying the bar."

"Roger that Banshee 1, and well done. Out."

Marshall contacted the airport and rolled in on final approach on a zero-zero-zero degree heading. He eased back on the throttle and greased the smoothest landing he had ever made.

He taxied over to the waiting line of emergency vehicles and one deuce-and-a-half Air Force truck. A soon as he rolled to a stop, technicians swarmed under the plane, popped open the bay door, and made off with the package. Delivery complete.

One hundred and twenty kilometers to the south, Bubba Spencer almost took the door with him as he sprinted from the radio room. Only guessing at the damage to his F-19, he gathered a box of tools and a few components from his service palette. Out in front of the hanger, he tossed an airman from an idling jeep and roared off to the north.

In an amazing display of skill, Bubba patched a few holes, repaired several fuel and hydraulic lines, and had the plane flyable again in four hours. It was imperative that they get the plane back to the safety of Ras Shaffaniyah before too many prying eyes could get a good look at it.

The exhausted sergeant collapsed back into the jeep and watched Marshall make his long roll to a one engine takeoff just as the harsh desert sun was beginning to peek over the horizon.

"I wonder if there's anyplace that could rustle me up some biscuits and gravy in Kuwait?"

The Stealth Pilot Papers
OPERATION:
Battering Ram

OPERATION: Battering Ram

The dim glow from the emergency lights refused to creep into the dark corners of the hardened aircraft hangar. An F-19 Stealth Fighter sat quietly under the cool red light in the center of the bay. Captain John "the Judge" Marshall sat sullenly in the far corner, leaning back against the wall in a metal folding chair. A close friend was dead. This was a side of combat he had not experienced before and he didn't like it, not one bit.

Marshall, and his squadron of Stealth Fighters named Team One–Furtim Vigilans (Covert Vigilantes), had been mobilized to Lakselv Airbase on the cold northern Norwegian coast two days ago, due to the increasing tensions between the USSR and Norway. After repeated warnings to the Soviets about incursions into their territorial waters, the Norwegian Navy isolated and then sank an intruding Soviet Victor III class nuclear powered attack sub. A trailing Soviet Alpha class sub responded by torpedoing three Norwegian ASW ships. Loss of life was heavy on both sides. The following day there were a number of border clashes. Most were minor firefights, but there were at least two locations where overeager Soviet officers had crossed the border and were now occupying Norwegian soil.

Fearing a massive NATO retaliation, the Soviets decided to make a preemptive strike against Norwegian airbases close to the border. Behind extreme radar jamming, a squadron of TU-95 Bear bombers managed to get close enough to launch a wave of AS-15 conventional cruise missiles. At Lakselv Airbase the F-15s scrambled in time to down three of the six incoming missiles, but three got through. Damage was light compared to other bases closer to the border, but one of the missiles scored a direct hit on an aircraft hangar. These concrete and steel hangars were designed to be tough but not to stand up to a direct hit from an AS-15. The resulting fire and explosion claimed sixteen lives, including an F-19 pilot and his crew chief.

That pilot was Marshall's closest friend. He had been his wingman when they flew F-111s together out of England. Together they had seen it all, from barfights in the back-alley dives of Subic Bay to the tapestry covered walls of Saudi Arabian palaces. They had flown side by side during the Tripoli raid in 1986, and now he was gone. All Marshall could think about was revenge against the Soviet air force. At dawn, he would get his opportunity.

Marshall stared right through the white cloud that hung in front of his face as his breath hit the cold air in the hangar. He didn't feel the chill as he imagined the targets for the coming operation. At dawn, 24 F-19s from four different airfields would stream across the border seeking targets on the Soviet Kola Peninsula. The Russians had been anticipating a night-time attack and seemed to relax when the low arctic sun finally appeared. It would cost them. Marshall had helped plan the raid and thus assigned to himself the targets he wanted. His beef was with the Soviet air force—it was payback time. The same squadron of TU-95s that had launched the attack against the airbases had been refitted with nuclear cruise missiles and was now orbiting menacingly behind the lines. It was an obvious warning for NATO to keep its distance.

But NATO Command in Brussels had planned a warning of its own, and Marshall and the F-19s were at the point of the spear. If all went according to plan, they would first take out the Bears and then select ground based targets, including radar sites as well as the circling IL-76 Mainstay AWACS aircraft. If successful, Operation Battering Ram would leave the door to the Kola Peninsula wide open for an air attack—an attack that wouldn't come if the Soviets could be forced to the bargaining table before this thing got too far out of hand.

One of the Bear bombers was circling over Kildenstroy, just south of Murmansk. Marshall visualized his Primary Target and played through the scenario again in his mind. For the twentieth time he saw the bright trail left by his missile and the moment of impact.

"Yo, Cap'n!" shouted the Crew Chief Bubba Spencer, who slammed the hangar door and jolted Marshall out of his reverie.

"Back here," answered the captain quietly, as the echoes of the sergeant's entrance faded away.

"The sun's about to peek over the hills, sir, time to saddle up and ride."

Marshall stood and strode slowly toward the aircraft. He passed the sergeant without saying a word, climbed up the metal ladder, and slipped into the cockpit. Bubba followed him up to help him strap in.

"Boss, you don't look so good. You ready for this one?"

"Bubba, this cockpit is my office. And when I'm in the office, I take care of business. Don't worry, I'll even the score today. Let's crank 'er up."

Just before a latecoming dawn at 0930, eight F-19s taxied from their hangers in unison and rolled towards the flight line. Without any radio chatter, each pilot took his place in line as they turned onto the runway. Marshall watched the parade with pride; these men were professionals, out to do a job. He rolled up next to another F-19 for the scheduled tandem take-off. The two aircraft in front of him rolled together down the runway, the roar of the engines only a distant hum through his canopy and helmet. When they left the ground and rolled to the right, Marshall and the other fighter started their takeoff roll. Without a word or a glance, the two aircraft stayed together as they flashed down the darkened runway, nosing up to leave the ground at the exact same moment. They leveled off at 500 feet and flew together for a few minutes. Then at ten kilometers from the base, Marshall looked over and gave a big thumbs up to his partner only 30 feet away. With that, he rolled to the left and the other plane rolled to the right, each now taking a lonely course to his distant target.

Marshall turned and pointed his plane due north, heading for the Norwegian Sea. Since his target was fairly close to the shore, he had chosen to use the amazing fuel efficiency of the F-19 to fly out over the water and parallel the coast, just out of radar detection range. The occasional chirps in his head-phones from the radar detection gear were the only sounds he heard as the F-19 weaved in between the hills. Already he was picking up signals from the big SA-12 site at Nikel, just across the border. Avoiding that site would take him way out over the Barents Sea, straining his limited fuel supply even with the extra tank he carried in one of his bays. The other bays were loaded with a full bag of Sidewinders, AMRAAMs, and MK 35 IN Incendiary Cluster Bombs. He planned on returning with all bays empty.

He crossed the rocky shore and turned slightly to the east. The signal from Nikel was coming in strong, so he backed off the throttle and settled down to 200 feet to reduce his radar signature. Checking the Tactical Display set on maximum range, Marshall noted that the aircraft carrier USS *Kennedy* and its protective group had moved into position north of Norway. "This is getting serious." The display showed a group of Navy F-18 Hornets flying CAP over the carrier.

When the signal from the SA-12 radar at Nikel finally started to fade, Marshall banked to the right and took a course parallel to the coastline, still bouncing along at low level. Two patrolling MiGs appeared on the display to the south, probably circling over Pechanga. As long as he stayed to the north they would pose no problem. Other aircraft occasionally popped up near the border—must be light attack aircraft in support of the ground troops. At this range he had no way of telling which side they were on. Gloved fingers clicked on the keyboard as Marshall activated the TrackCam in air-to-ground mode. The first thing to show up on the small CRT was a Soviet Krivak-class destroyer steaming west, just north of the huge port at Murmansk. It was not broadcasting radar, but he would have to keep an eye on it. Some of the newer ones carried a very effective doppler system.

Marshall worked his head from side to side. Though he had yet to encounter the enemy, the long distance low-level flight had placed a great deal of stress on the pilot. A computer generated message flashed up on the HUD, WAYPOINT 2 REACHED. He was due north of Murmansk and eased the stick to the right to start a gentle turn inland.

Marshall relished this mission. He had managed to arrange it so both of his assigned targets were part of the Soviet air force. He had lost track of the big picture. He just wanted retribution. His right hand caressed the stick as he bounced in the turbulence at 150 feet. The cool white lights on his HUD showed Heading 170, Speed 203, Altitude 155. Maybe he was crazy to be doing this, but he was also extremely good at it.

He approached the Soviet coastline about halfway between the port cities Murmansk and Severomorsk, dipping closer to the deck to avoid a small SA-2 battery. The white sands of the shoreline blazed in the early morning sun as Marshall went "feet dry" over the craggy landscape. Taking a deep breath, he tried not to think too much about the seriousness of flying a combat mission against the Soviet Union. He switched the HUD to air-to-air mode and began to scan for his target. Marshall's racing heart beat even faster when three aircraft appeared on the Tactical Display circling over Kildenstroy. "Okay, let's sort out who's who." He adjusted the TrackCam to lock onto the closest target. A perfect picture of a lazily turning MiG-31 snapped onto the CRT. A quick keystroke switched the camera to the next target, which turned out to be a SU-27. "Just a couple of high-priced baby sitters." Marshall switched the camera again and the huge TU-95 Bear bomber flashed onto the screen under the words PRIMARY TARGET.

Marshall's fist tightened around the stick, as he fought the urge to go to full power and rush the attack. A quick scan of the instruments showed all systems to be nominal as he selected an AMRAMM missile. A quick red flash on the EMV scale caught his attention. He had been hit by a very strong radar signal—not strong enough to detect him yet, but enough to worry about. A new symbol appeared on the Tactical Display and he requested further information on the radar site from the computer. OVER THE HORIZON DOPPLER RADAR SYSTEM—LOCATION KIROVSK, was the reply. The next pulse from this site was even stronger, three-quarters of the way down the scale, and Marshall was heading right towards it.

Marshall gritted his teeth. "This puts a whole new twist on things." Between pulses, he banked the aircraft hard and pulled out on a course heading of 200. He could maintain that course and not get any closer to Kirovsk and still close on the target over Kildenstroy. The range to the Bear was closing fast. Just 40 km and he still had not been spotted. It didn't stand a chance.

At 36 kilometers, the words TARGET LOCKED appeared

on the CRT. Marshall moved in for the kill. Slowing to a mere 140 knots, he managed to avoid the strong radar searches of the circling fighters.

An AMRAMM missile is launched with that Bear Bomber's name on it.

Like a big cat stalking its prey, Marshall moved slowly, hugging the ground until just the right moment. When the range closed to 20 km, he pounced with lightning quickness and ferocious force. Pushing the throttle to the stops, he quickly gathered the speed he would need to engage the Bear and its escorts. When the range closed to 16 km, the Targeting circle turned bright red and Marshall reefed back on the stick to bring the higher-flying Bear into the middle of the missile envelope. The bay doors whined open and he squeezed the trigger unleashing an AMRAAM. Marshall felt the aircraft shudder as the aircraft hunting missile flared off the rail. Now at high speed and clear of the ground clutter, the F-19 was just another fighter, very vulnerable to radar detection. The flash of the air-to-air missile was seen by the bomber pilot, who started a diving turn down into the clouds to try and escape. The two fighters turned towards the F-19, but Marshall locked them up and put them on the defensive with a missile aimed at each.

Marshall looked back over his shoulder and followed the white trail left by the first missile. The lumbering Bear twisted and turned but could not shake the agile missile. Thirty feet away from the Bear's undercarriage, the proximity fuse detonated and ripped the belly of the aircraft open. The bomber started to tumble and then exploded with a flash, disappearing into the clouds. Gone so quickly.

The two fighters were still turning hard to avoid the incoming missiles. Marshall kept them on the defensive with a closer-range Sidewinder shot at each and then dove for the deck and safety. He cut the throttle and tried his best to disappear, screeching over a wheat field at less than 100 feet. He felt a deep satisfaction when a message came up on the HUD telling him both of the fighters had gone down in flames.

Three-hundred kilometers away back over Norway, the operators in the E-3A Sentry AWACS plane also felt satisfaction as one by one, the Bear bombers blinked off the radar screens. The oddly shaped Stealth Fighters had once again proved their worth and eliminated the cruise missile threat. But there was still more to do.

Marshall knew he would have to act quickly now if he was going to complete his secondary mission. The elite MiG-31 fighter wing at nearby Kilpyaur would be scrambling due to his attack on the bomber, and Marshall wanted to catch them on the ground. He switched to air-to-ground mode and scanned until he found the airfield and the nearby SA-5 SAM site; the SAM would be a problem. Only 30 kilometers away, the site was close to picking him up, but not quite yet. He headed straight for it, keeping low. Radar energy from the old pulse system hit him again, but not enough reflected back for the operators to detect him.

At ten miles out he turned hard back towards the airfield. BONK! The next pulse flashed all the way down the scale and got him. One more and they would have a good track. But it was too late. The airfield was only five kilometers away. Marshall armed and readied the Mk 35 Cluster Bomb Units and lined up the runway for his approach. At 3 klicks out he popped up to 500 feet, punched open the bay doors, and then hit the pickle button to drop a CBU as the busy airfield flashed underneath him. Numerous taxiing aircraft and roving fuel and ammo trucks were in plain view. Once it left the F-19's bay, the CBU broke open and spread hundreds of baseball-sized incendiary bomblets over several hundred square yards. Whatever they hit was immediately covered with burning liquid. This included the fuel trucks and armed and fueled aircraft waiting to take off.

A fire storm swept across the base. Fuel trucks exploded, sending sheets of burning JP fuel in all directions. Dozens of aircraft were damaged either by the sticky burning liquid or by the resulting explosions. As the fire grew, exploding ordnance that cooked off due to the heat forced the firefighters out of the area. There was nothing they could do but watch it burn. This fighter wing would be out of operation for the duration. "Secondary Target destroyed."

But the SA-5 SAM site was not caught in the fire and quickly sent a large SA-5 Gammon missile racing after the intruder. Marshall noticed the missile lock right away and turned hard to get the missile broadside to him. At almost mach three the SAM ate up the range quickly. Marshall punched out a decoy drone and let out a deep breath as the SAM passed safely behind him. But he was not out of the woods yet. The decoy would die out in another couple of seconds, giving the SAM crew another shot. So rather than turn away from the site, Marshall headed back towards it with a high-G climbing turn. Marshall let out a low groan as his body weight was suddenly multiplied by five. Just as the decoy gave out, the Track light came on again, but Marshall was doing some tracking of his own. Before the crew could launch another Gammon missile, he streaked over the site and covered it with another load of burning bomblets. The remaining five missiles caught fire and cooked off on their launchers, aiding the destruction of the main guidance radar.

Other F-19s had been equally successful with their targets. The two Soviet Il-72 airborne controllers were both quieted with U.S.-made missiles. But there were still a large number of fighters in the air, and without their airborne controllers, they were desperately looking for something to shoot. The fire at the airbase sent a huge cloud of smoke and fire into the air, which drew fighters to the area like moths to a flame. Suddenly the air around Captain Marshall became very crowded.

With MiGs closing in from the north, south, and west, Marshall took a second to consider his situation. A quick runthrough of his weapons showed only two Sidewinder missiles, but he still had a full magazine of cannon shells. He figured he might have time to sneak back to the north and out over the water but he wanted a shot at the Soviet air force, and what looked like half of it was headed his way. Besides, with their IL-76 aircraft gone, he had an advantage—he could see them and they couldn't see him.

A check in air-to-air mode showed six incoming aircraft. Two MiG-29 Fulcrums from the west, two SU-27 Flankers from the south, and two Yak-38 Forgers from the north. Marshall was surprised to see the Yaks—the Kiev aircraft carrier must be in port. With only two missiles left, he decided to go after the MiG-29s first, though they were only slightly more dangerous than the SU-27s. The lowly Yaks, on the other hand, should not be a problem.

Marshall turns to face the incoming MiGs.

Marshall weaved around so the MiGs would pass by on his right. He stayed down on the deck in the early morning shadows, feeling very exposed operating in the daytime. He had planned to whip around on the tails of the MiGs as they passed for a classic rear quarter shot, but a check of the TrackCam showed they were probably closing too fast. By the time he could swing the F-19 around, they would be moving out of the Sidewinder's effective envelope. Besides, it looked like the two Flankers would cross his path first. The slower Yaks were lagging behind.

"Let's try it this way then." Marshall heaved the fighter over onto its side and turned hard toward the SU-27s. Increasing the throttle, his oxygen mask pressed back into his face as he held the turn to keep his nose ahead of the closest fighter in a good lead-pursuit position. At over 1000 knots closure, the Soviet fighter grew rapidly in his windscreen. He was surprised they hadn't picked him up on radar yet; the next pulse might get him, but he would be past them soon.

In a perfect lead-pursuit position, Marshall bears down on a bogey.

It happened very quickly. As the Flankers sped in from the left, Marshall held his lead on the fighters and then pressed the trigger to send a sheet of explosive shells out in front of them. As they flashed by in front of him, the lead aircraft nosed right through the stream of gunfire and exploded. Marshall grimaced as he flew right through the pall of smoke left in the air, not knowing what debris he might be sucking into his engines. He jammed the throttle forward and slid behind the other flanker. Yanking the aircraft over again, he turned to face the two MiGs that had passed behind him during the gunfight. They were both turning hard to come back and investigate, having seen the Flanker cartwheel into the ground. A bright blue flash on the EMV scale and a warning tone told Marshall that within a couple of seconds all the aircraft would know his position. The two MiGs pulled out of the turn headed straight for the F-19. But the "Judge" was quicker on the draw and sent a Sidewinder racing after each plane.

Meanwhile, the other SU-27 had maneuvered around onto Marshall's tail and announced his presence with an AA-8 Aphid heat-seeking missile. Marshall put the F-19 into a shallow dive to pick up airspeed. The throttle was already all the way forward. Even with the F-19's reduced IR signature, the AA-8 had no trouble locking onto the fighter and quickly made up ground. The airspeed indicator on the HUD was counting up past 450 knots when the Missile Proximity Klaxon sounded. Impact was just seconds away. Marshall punched out two flares, flicked on the IR jammer, and pulled a six-G turn to the right. He grunted and tightened his abdominal muscles to try and keep his blood from pooling in his legs. Even so, the world went to black and white as the blood left his head. The Flashing red *I* indicating missile lock blinked off for a moment, fooled momentarily by the countermeasures. But it quickly reappeared, flashing steadily in the corner of Marshall's right eye. Marshall held his turn, concentrating through his tunnel vision, still fighting against the mounting Gs. Finally the Flashing *I* went off. The countermeasures had fooled the missile just long enough so it was late following the F-19's turn, forcing it to eventually overshoot.

Marshall finds himself in a catfight with MiGs and missiles.

The MiGs were not so fortunate. The new M-generation Sidewinders bore right through the trail of flares left by the fleeing fighters and stayed padlocked onto the hot engines. They exploded only a second apart and sent the two fighters trailing smoke into the ground.

The other flanker was still behind Marshall; it fired off another AA-8, which never locked on. The F-19's hard turn had bled off a lot of airspeed, and the Flanker pilot struggled to slow up and stay behind the oddly shaped fighter. The range had closed to less than a kilometer. Marshall jinked his plane wildly, trying to stay out of the Flanker's gunsights. He jerked quickly to his right and then back hard to the left. The Flanker pilot did not react quickly enough and wound up heading to the right while Marshall was turning left. The Soviet pilot quickly reversed his turn to follow the F-19, but Marshall reversed his turn also, once again catching the Soviet going the wrong way. The Soviet realized his mistake too late. As he turned hard to get back on the F-19's tail, Marshall cut power and extended the speed brake. The Flanker pilot watched helplessly as the F-19 slowed up quickly and slid underneath him. Marshall's perfectly timed scissor maneuver had caused the Flanker to overshoot above him. He used what little airspeed he had to bring the nose of the aircaft up for a quick gun shot at the scrambling Flanker.

"You're a mort!" He only got off one burst before the aircraft stalled and nosed back down. But with the range only a couple hundred yards it was enough. The short-range burst took one of the Flanker's horizontal stabilizers off at the base and raked the belly of the aircraft, causing an immediate hydraulic failure. The Soviet took the wise move and optioned for a silk-assisted landing. Marshall saw the chute bloom open to his right as he successfully battled to pull the Stealth Fighter out of the stall.

The slow Yak-38s were just now arriving. The worried pilots had witnessed the numerous explosions and now could not raise their comrades on the radio. Their pathetic radars did not give them a clue as to the F-19's whereabouts. They flew in slowly and surveyed the damage. The airbase and the SAM radar site were still ablaze, and four smoking craters marked the impact points of the other Soviet fighters. The pilot of the lead Forger hoped that whatever had done all this was gone. His VTOL Yak-38 was not much of a fighter. It was heavy, slow, and had an outdated fire control system, certainly no match for a MiG-29 or anything that could shoot one down.

The pair flew in a relatively loose formation with about a half kilometer separation. They were busily reporting what they had seen back to the ship and not keeping as close a watch on each other's tail as they should have been. Marshall swung around behind a small group of hills at low level and approached one of the slow moving Yaks from the rear. Without letting the Yak wingman give a word of warning, the F-19 pulled up from low level onto the Yak's tail and sprayed it with cannon fire. A frantic radio call for help came too late. Fire warning lights flashed, warning klaxons blared in the Forger's cockpit, and engine output dropped to almost nothing. The pilot just had time to look over his shoulder and watch his wingman turn hard away and dive for speed. He shook his head and reached between his legs for the eject handle.

The second bogey turns hard and heads for home.

Marshall watched the other Yak beat feet, headed back to the ship. He thought about pursuing the fleeing aircraft, but a quick check of the fuel gauge told him that would not be a good idea. Besides, there were other fighters headed in from the south. It was time to make a graceful exit.

He cut the throttles and headed back down to low altitude. A check of the Map Display showed a lot of radar activity due north, between Murmansk and Pechenga. So he turned to a 035-degree heading, which would take him back through the gap between Murmansk and Severomorsk. He activated the extra fuel tank he was carrying and pumped the contents into the main fuel cell. "Maybe taking on those fighters wasn't such a good idea after all." He ran it through the computer again, but it came out the same way. He might not have enough fuel to get home.

Back out over the water, he headed due north for a while and then back to the west. He pulled up to 500 feet whenever there was no danger of radar in the area. The smoother ride there should help his fuel economy. But the indicator on the fuel gauge seemed to be marching double-time towards the bottom of the scale. He pulled out his briefing notes and looked for a closer airstrip of any sort. But Lakselv was it. Even the highways were covered with snow and ice. Then a germ of an idea started to grow in his head. "Nah, I don't even want to *think* about that!" But as the minutes clicked off the digital clock and the engines sucked up more fuel, it didn't look like he had a choice. He pulled out his charts and notes, looking for the radio frequency and call sign for the aircraft carrier USS *Kennedy*.

He didn't get very far with the air boss on the carrier, so he contacted the ever watchful E-3A Sentry AWACS plane and explained his situation. The F-19 did have a hook to catch the arresting cable on the carrier's deck. And he had done carrier landings in practice, although never on an actual carrier. He always figured any mission that required carrier operations would be flown by one of the three former Navy pukes in his squadron. Never in his wildest nightmares did he think he would actually have to land on a carrier some day. But the carrier was 60 kilometers closer than the base and reachable. It was that or ditch a 60 million dollar aircraft and risk freezing to death in the Arctic Ocean.

The AWACS controller came back on the radio and told Marshall he'd convinced the carrier to let him try a landing. He asked if he wanted the carrier to raise the crash barrier to catch him. But the cables in the barrier would total his fragile aircraft just as surely as if he had dropped it in the ocean. No way. He said he would try and catch the cable.

The *Kennedy* agreed to let the captain try and land. They turned into the wind on a 180-degree heading. Marshall would have to come around and land from the north, straining his limited fuel even further. He adjusted his course to take him 20 kilometers north of the *Kennedy*. Easing up to 1000 feet, he settled into a smooth flight at 200 knots. Once he was almost due north of the ship, he turned back hard and lined up on a 180-degree heading with the ship dead ahead. He activated the Instrument Landing System and lowered his landing gear. The ILS would give him the proper glidepath to follow to hit the deck. Ten kilometers out he started a gentle descent waiting for the glidepath indicator to catch up with him. The inside of the small fighter suddenly got hot and sticky as he fought to keep the tiny carrier deck lined up. When he intercepted the glidepath, he cut his throttle and let the nose down a little to keep the bar in the center of the scale. "Jeez, I'm coming in steep!" A carrier approach was much steeper than normal, and it had been awhile since he had practiced one. The Low Fuel Warning Light on his console started to flash—he would only get one pass at this.

Sweat poured down his face and his heart raced as the deck climbed towards him. The cables became visible and he pointed his nose right at them. "This is really crazy!" He could see the rescue helicopters hovering off to the side of the ship, waiting for him to put it in the drink. The ondeck betting was probably furious.

Three kilometers out and the deck loomed in front of him, he still pointed his nose right at the cables. Two kilometers . . . one . . . there was no turning back now. Just when it looked as if he would plow nose first into the deck, he opened the speed brake and pulled the nose up.

Marshall catches the cable on his very first carrier landing attempt. Sierra Hotel!

WHAM! The whole aircraft shook as the gear slammed into the deck. Marshall felt like he had been dropped out of a second-story window in a recliner. He jammed the throttles forward, not knowing if he had caught the cable or not. Then suddenly he hit a brick wall; at least that's what it felt like. The hook caught the cable and the aircraft went from 160 knots to 0 in a fraction of a second. Marshall was thrown forward against his straps and momentarily dazed by the sudden stop.

When his eyeballs stopped spinning, there was a smiling face with an odd headset pounding on the canopy next to him. He had done it! He had actually landed on a carrier! Regaining his wits, he opened the canopy and was helped down as the deck crew attached a small tractor to the front wheel of the F-19 to tow it to the hangar elevator. Marshall was greeted by a smiling group of the deck crew. Thumbs up and back slaps all around. The commander of the carrier's air group, with CAG across the front of his blue baseball cap, cut his way through the crowd to Marshall and led him to a hatchway in the island structure. Once in the quieter hallways of the carrier, the CAG gave Marshall a smile and a wink. "Not half bad for an Air Force puke!"

Not half bad for an Air Force puke!

The helicopter ride from the *Kennedy* back to Lakselv had been long and cold. Marshall was the last pilot to arrive back at the base. By the time he was finished with his debriefing, the party in the Officers' Club was well underway. All of the pilots had made it back safely, and each was carving up the air with his hands as he explained his heroics in great detail.

When Marshall stuck his weary but smiling face through the door, a loud cheer went up over the already noisy party. It was obvious to everyone that Marshall and his crew chief had already started celebrating, as someone had painted eight red stars on the side of his face, one for each Soviet aircraft he had downed. Marshall leaped in the door letting out a hoot and clutching something tightly in both fists. A voice from the end of the bar yelled out, "The Judge is cleared for landing, call the ball," giving him the standard aircraft carrier landing clearance.

Marshall yelled back, "Roger, the Judge has the ball!" And with that he took three long strides, stepped up and off the back of a colonels's chair, and launched himself head-first towards the dripping bar top. He made a perfect carrier landing on his belly and slid the length of the bar with his arms outstretched, scattering bottles and pilots in all directions. The "fire crew" immediately arrived to douse his flames with the contents of their glasses. Another cheer went up when Marshall sat up and showed his buddies what he was clutching so tightly in each fist: a letter from the wing commander recommending him for the Air Force Cross and a new set of major's insignia. It would be quite a party.

Appendices

Appendix A
Getting the Graphic for the Real Stealth Fighter— the F-117A

While MicroProse was developing *F-19 Stealth Fighter*, everyone in the industry really believed the real Stealth Fighter would be designated the F-19. The general shape of the aircraft was also pretty much agreed to be bell shaped, much like the space shuttle.

On the very day MicroProse announced the release of *F-19*, November 10, 1988, the Air Force made an announcement of its own. On that day it released the first photo of the real Stealth Fighter and announced it would be designated the F-117A.

Well, the game was already set to ship, so it was too late to change the graphic and the name. But for those of you who insist on accuracy, there's a graphic of the F-117A you can download from the CompuServe online service. The file is located in the Gamepub Forum in Library 13.

For those of you who don't have access to CompuServe, newer versions of the game will probably include this file. Then, if you like, you can switch this file for the F-19 graphics file. Doing so will allow you to see the F-117A when using the External Views.

Appendix B
Updating *F-19 Stealth Fighter*

Though you probably haven't noticed them, there were a few bugs in the original version of *F-19 Stealth Fighter* and room for a little improvement. The original version was 435.01, and now an updated version numbered 435.03 has been released. Version 435.04 should follow soon—it will probably be the last update. It should be out by the time you read this. You can locate the version number of your software by looking on the copyright screen when the game first boots up.

Besides taking care of a few rarely noticed bugs and compatibility with certain clones, the improvements in this version are:

• The inclusion of missions starting and ending on a Navy carrier at all game levels. Previously, you had to acquire a very high point total in order to qualify for carrier missions. You needed somewhere in the range of 70,000 total points and the missions were only offered in the Lybian scenario.
• A low-altitude warning klaxon.
• The ability to set the climb angle ladder so it's on at all times.

An update program has been set up as follows:

If your version is still under the 90-day warranty, you can return the original disks and have them updated free.

Otherwise you can send $10 and the original disks for updating. Or, if you still have the Request for Backup Copy Form in your box, you can send that in with $10 for a completely updated backup copy.

If you have other questions about getting the updated version you should call MicroProse Customer Service at (301) 771-1151.

Suggested Reading List

If you would like to read more about the Stealth Fighter and its role in the modern Air Force, I would suggest the following:

Sweetman, Bill. *Stealth Aircraft*. Osceola, Wisconsin: Motorbooks International 1986.

    A good introduction to stealth concepts, though somewhat outdated now.

Jones, Joseph. *Stealth Technology: The Art of Black Magic*. Blue Ridge Summit, PA: Tab Books 1989.

    An excellent introduction to all kinds of stealth-type aircraft with the latest unclassified material.

Clancy, Tom. *Red Storm Rising*. New York: G.P. Putnam's Sons 1986.

    Although this is a work of fiction, it provides an outstanding example of how the Stealth Fighter might actually be used in combat in "Operation Dreamland." A "must read" for military simulation fans.